HOW TO BE

BRILLIANT

BRAINPOWER FOR KIDS

SOMEBODY NEEDED TO MAKE IT SIMPLE, EASY, PRACTICAL, FUN, AND DOABLE.

To Sandi,
Thank you so much
David Howell

DAVID HOWELL

THIS IS NOT YOUR TYPICAL BRAIN BOOK.

How To Be Brilliant – Brainpower For Kids

Copyright © 2020 by David Howell.

For information contact:

CS@HowToBeBrilliant.com

http://www.HowToBeBrilliant.com

Published by Blak Dog Group LLC

ISBN-10 : 1-7348340-1-3

ISBN-13 : 978-1-7348340-1-7

First Edition: June 2020

10 9 8 7 6 5 4 3 2 1

DISCLAIMER

The content of this book is for informational and entertainment purposes only. It is not meant to be a substitute for professional medical or psychological advice, diagnosis, or treatment. Always seek the advice of your physician or other qualified health provider with any questions you may have regarding a medical or mental health condition or suspected condition. Never disregard or delay seeking professional medical or psychological advice.

The author and publisher of this book are not liable or responsible in any manner whatsoever to any person or entity for any loss, damage, injury, death, or any other adverse consequence of any nature, past, present or future, that may result from or is alleged to have resulted from studying, practicing, applying or misusing any of the concepts, techniques, or ideas and/or from following any information or instructions contained within this book.

If you choose to engage in any of the activities described in this book or utilize any of the information in this book, you do so at your own risk.

CONTENTS

This book is dedicated to the two

most brilliant people I know:

Garrett and Jenna

1

FREQUENTLY ASKED QUESTIONS

Let's get some of your questions answered right now.

Well, this is weird. A FAQ as the first chapter of a book? Sure. You undoubtedly have questions. Why shouldn't I answer them now? And being conventional is so overrated.

ARE YOU JUST GOING TO SAY WHAT THE EXPERTS SAY?

Most of the time, no. I'm often going to fly right in the face of what you've been led to believe. The "experts" tend to complicate things and to focus on groundbreaking new methods and the like. I'm going to simplify things and focus on working with how your child's brain is designed to work. That's neither complicated nor groundbreaking.

I'm also not going to tell you that helping your child develop and use intelligence is best left to strangers with letters after their names. You know your child better than anyone on the planet. You've got this and so has your child.

WHY SHOULD I EVEN DO THIS?

Many people are nearly stimulus-response beings. That might sound a little harsh but it's true. Our children are becoming conditioned to not think. Intelligence and thinking are under assault by an education system that isn't even interested in intelligence (lots more on that in chapter 4), devices that do our thinking for us, and ubiquitous entertainment that wastes our potential. You should do this to fight back and to protect, and even enhance, your child's intelligence.

WHAT AGE GROUP IS THIS BOOK FOR?

This book is primarily for the early years, before school, because those are the most formative years. Nearly all the content can be adapted for later years as well, right up through high school and college. That covers a lot of time and a lot of stages. So, some of the material you will be able to apply immediately, and some will need to wait a bit. Some of you, who have older children, will need to play catchup. Every child is different as well, so success depends greatly on you, the parent or guardian, for guidance and implementation. Don't worry, it's actually easy and even fun.

Much of the content is focused on the early years because that is the time when you have the most interaction with your child and it is the time when your child's "normal" is established. It's also the time that you have the most influence on your child. Hopefully, your child will start school as late as possible which will give maximum time for building a foundation of brilliance.

WHAT DO YOU MEAN BY YOUR CHILD'S "NORMAL?"

By "normal" I simply mean that which is normal for you, your child, and your household. I could just as easily call it your "typical." For example, we never played video games in our home (we did have a Wii* but only for interactive sports), and we never drank sodas. We didn't forbid anything, there were no hard and fast rules, and there was zero drama. That's because we just lived our "normal." My kids are now 18 and 20, and they still have zero desire to play video games, and neither of them has ever drank a soda. They're just living our normal.

WHAT DOES THIS BOOK COVER?

This book covers the very basics of brilliance. This is the beginning. This is all about setting the stage and building your child's intellectual foundation. The earlier you start, the better. If your children are already beyond those formative early years don't despair. All of this will work for them as well. It will even work for adults. It's just a little more difficult in later years because it's easier to create your normal than it is to change to a new normal. But don't worry about any of that. As I like to say, "You can't start any earlier than now."

IS THIS AN EXHAUSTIVE MANUAL?

Heck no. This book is about the first steps and it is focused primarily on building a foundation of brilliance upon which all future endeavors will stand. Again, this is just the basics, but those basics are extremely important and powerful. As your child grows up, specific skills for acquiring knowledge and specific skills for knowledge utilization will need to be added relative to your child's specific goals. Those would include academic skills such as studying and test-taking, social skills, communication skills, problem-solving skills, memory skills, and creative skills just to name a very few. All of that will be much easier with the foundation of brilliance firmly constructed.

*Wii is a registered trademark of Nintendo of America Inc.

CAN A PARENT DO THIS?

None of this is difficult. In fact, it can not only be easy, it can be fun! The "experts" would have you believe that helping your children learn to develop and use their intelligence is beyond you. They're the only ones capable because they have the education necessary. Well, much of that education of theirs is the problem, rather than the answer.

You are fully capable. That's because helping your children become brilliant is mostly about preventing them from losing the abilities they naturally have. That's right. It's already there, right in their fantastically powerful little brains. Your children are already capable of brilliance. All we need to do is ensure that they use it and that they don't lose it.

I'm going to show you deceptively easy ways to help your child not only maintain their brilliance but take it to much higher levels than you may have imagined. And it will be you that takes them there. At the same time, you will become closer to your child, and you may learn a little yourself.

Everything I'm going to tell you is natural, effective, normal, and powerful. In fact, much of it is exactly what has powered many of the greatest minds in history that all the other brain books like to talk about. The challenge is that you are going to have to let go of some of the beliefs that have been pounded into your head by everyone from your friends to your family to the education system. Just because it's accepted doesn't mean it's right.

IS MY CHILD GOING TO BE PERFECT?

No! That's delusional. Perfection is not even a reasonable goal. Brilliant people make mistakes just like everyone else. Becoming and being brilliant means trying new things and taking risks. That means failure is inevitable. High expectations can be very motivating. Unreasonable expectations can be disastrous, leading to fear of failure, hopelessness, or worse. Let your child be human.

WILL MY CHILD HAVE A LIFELONG LOVE OF LEARNING?

Maybe. Maybe not. Your child will probably develop a lifelong love of thinking though. My two kids (daughter 18 and son 20) are definitely brilliant. They've nearly maxed out every standardized test they've ever taken, they have been top of their class since first grade, they have lifelong 4.0 GPA's (including their college coursework), my son was a certified industry level C++ programmer at 15, my daughter's hobby since age 13 has been quantum physics, and they both don't like school, schoolwork, and even reading. Wow, that was a long sentence. I homeschooled them from the 6th and 8th grades, and we rarely spent more than 2½ hours on school in a day, and I never assigned homework. That was still more schooltime than they wanted. They don't live for studying. But, and this is a big but, they do love to think, and they love to accomplish. What they despise is anything slow-paced and useless which pretty much sums up a typical school day.

WILL MY CHILD BECOME A GENIUS?

Probably not. True geniuses are anomalies. It may be possible to create genius-level performance in specific areas of interest by grooming a child from near infancy, but would any sane person want to do that? Genius also has its downsides. Often, those of genius-level intellect have difficulty relating to others and the world we take for granted. Brilliant people, on the other hand, are very intelligent but well-adjusted and well adapted as well.

However, even brilliant people can have some difficulty relating to and tolerating those of lesser intelligence. There is some truth to the old adage, "Ignorance is bliss."

WHY NOT WAIT AND LET SCHOOL HANDLE IT?

First, school isn't going to get this done. In fact, school is the enemy of brilliance (see chapter 4). Second, you would be missing out on a tremendous opportunity. During the early years, from birth to age five, your child's brain experiences its greatest growth and neuron interconnection development. Those are the most valuable years for developing your child's brilliance. Also, during these important formative years, you have your child's attention more than you likely ever will.

IS THIS A PARENTING BOOK?

No. Am I going to discuss a lot of what you do as a parent? Yes. You're the person who is going to make this happen. I'm going to teach you about intelligence. It's up to you and your child how that intelligence is used. I'm going to tell you *how* your child should think, not *what* you or your child should think.

WHY ISN'T THIS BOOK FILLED WITH STUDY REFERENCES?

By now, you're realizing that this is not your typical highbrow, formal, textbook-like book about intelligence. That's because I want it to be a relatable, usable, practical book that enables you to make things happen. I didn't write this to wow you with my brilliance and dazzle you with endless peer-reviewed journal article citations. However, you will encounter a few article references where they're necessary. When I do cite a study, it will be one that has been reliably replicated or one that I believe is very relevant to the discussion. Heck, there's one in the next paragraph.

The psychology world is in what has been termed a "replication crisis." The problem is that many attempts to replicate well known and accepted concepts from past studies have failed to yield similar results. In 2014 a project called "Many Labs 2" was undertaken by 186 psychologists around the world in an attempt to replicate 28 classic findings from earlier studies. Half of those attempts failed, "According to a strict significance criterion (p < .0001), 14 (50%) of the 28 replications still provided such evidence" (Klein 477). This is a big part of why I rely more on your knowledge of your child as an individual augmented by additional ideas which you may apply, observe, and assess very personally in your life and circumstances.

WHY DO YOU THINK EVERYONE ELSE HAS IT WRONG?

Not everyone is wrong. There have been many great minds who have sounded the alarm over the dumb way we "educate" children for many decades. That's because anyone who has even a rudimentary understanding of the human mind can see from a hundred yards away, in the dark, on a foggy night, with their eyes closed that the way we do it just plain doesn't match up with how human beings learn and think. Even the psychological community understands that and a lot of them have been very vocal about it for decades, to no avail. I have my own reasons for believing that our way of educating is wrong that you can read about in chapter 4.

ARE THERE DOWNSIDES TO BEING BRILLIANT?

There sure are. Peer pressure from those who feel threatened by your child's intellect, being easily bored, a tendency to overthink, a lowered tolerance for stupidity, and noticing every double negative uttered by everyone on the planet to name a few. Being a perfectionist is common too.

WHY IS THERE NO CHAPTER ON MEMORY?

Memory skill development for an adult, like you are probably envisioning, is very different than for your child. For an adult, it involves very specific tasks and goals. Conversely, memory development for your child, especially very young children, is based on development and preservation of broad and general aspects of intelligence, thinking, and habit development. Simply relying on one's brain for memory, rather than technology, helps solidify the habits that support a robust memory. In chapters 6 through 12, you will learn ways to preserve and build upon the innate brilliance that came with your child's birth. Development of a powerful memory will be a natural result of that process.

Of course, specific skills will be needed during school years and into adulthood that will augment and utilize the brilliance developed in these very young years. I will discuss those memory skills in following volumes on such topics as how to study, test-taking, and brilliance for adults. For now, avoid tricks and methods as they are mostly useless, and they definitely do not contribute to development of natural intelligence for a child.

HOW ABOUT OLDER KIDS AND ADULTS?

Everything in this book applies to anyone who has a brain. The big difference is that this book focuses on creating habits that contribute to brilliance in those very early formative years. Those habits form without conscious effort and with ease when children are very young, before the brain's frontal lobes have fully developed (more on that later). For older kids and adults those habits must form due to deliberate action and conscious, analytical thought which is not nearly as easy. Certainly doable. Just not as easy.

2

BRAINPOWER SHOULDN'T BE DIFFICULT

Why does everyone complicate it so much?

REALLY! IT'S THE BRAIN YOUR CHILD WAS born with. It shouldn't be difficult to use. There have been countless books written that claim they will help you release your, or your child's, inner genius. They range from painfully academic to strangely metaphysical to just plain snake oil. Mind maps, accelerated learning, affirmations, right-brain left-brain synergy, neuroplasticity, puzzles and quizzes, ESP, autosuggestion, speed reading, mediation, mnemonics, listening to Mozart, mantras, relaxation techniques and the like are just a few of the methods and concepts they promote.

Those books nearly all follow the same structure. First, they wow you with amazing descriptions of the brain and the intricacies of its internal workings. Then it's on to the obligatory list of the greatest memorizers of all time. Sprinkle in discussion of a few historical geniuses for good measure. Then they explain their methods which they believe will enable you, or your child, to become a genius.

There's a huge, devastating, glaring problem though. What they teach is nearly always so convoluted, complicated, impractical, and time-consuming that it is impossible to implement in your daily life much less a child's life. Really, what good is information if you can't put it to work? And it would be nice if we could skip some of the useless detail. That's the gap I'm here to fill although I do have to include some boring background info. Sorry.

Now, if you are like me and you enjoy all that detail, those books are out there ready to occupy your bathroom time for weeks or even months. Really, some of it is fascinating stuff, even if a lot of it is useless.

WELL... THEN WHAT IS THIS BOOK ABOUT?

This book is intended to be doable and effective above all else. The surest way to accomplish that is to work with your child's natural way of learning. This is a basic, everyday guide on how to help your child become brilliant. Not a genius, brilliant. To better understand what it means to be brilliant (see chapter 3).

However!
This is not a step-by-step instruction manual. Every child is different. Every family is different. Every child develops differently. Helping your child develop, and utilize, intelligence is an everchanging process. Cookie-cutter instructions will be useless for all but the very basics. You must observe your child's progress constantly and adapt as needed. But don't worry. As I keep saying, it's easy.

The methods in this book utilize many of the same principles that are discussed in those other books but without droning on and on about it (I just drone on and on about it being easy). Yeah, I do have to include some detail and some base knowledge because you need to know the why behind the method and to convince you (if you're not already convinced) that your child's brain can do much more than it's probably doing now. The overriding emphasis, though, is on helping you make it happen.

NOW FOR THE GROUNDBREAKING GENIUS STUFF! NOPE.

If there were some magical way to turn your child into a genius, don't you think you would have heard about it by now? I firmly believe you can help your child become more intelligent, much more intelligent. No, we're not going to change your child's genetic potential. We don't need to.

It's kind of like trained seals at an aquarium (not that I condone that). I really hate keeping them captive for entertainment, but the analogy still works. The seals do all sorts of fascinating tricks to the amazement of the audience. Spoiler alert! If you listen closely to the trainer's presentation before the show starts (who does that, right?), you will hear the trainer explain that the seals will do nothing that isn't natural behavior. No, the seals are not performing tricks. They will tell you that they don't teach the seals anything new. "How can that possibly be? They jumped through hoops, balanced balls on their noses, beached themselves in front of the crowd, and they waved hi to my three-year-old."

The trainers will explain that they elicit natural behaviors and abilities on command. They simply get the seals to do what they do. They just throw in a few toys, props, and situations that us humans can relate to. The seals are at their most efficient when they are just doing what they do. There's nothing out of their skillset and they're not having to think about what they're doing. That's what brilliant people do. They get their brain to do what it naturally does. Most of the time it's automatic, like a seal in the wild. Other times it's on command for a specific purpose, like when they need to jump through a mental hoop. The only difference between brilliant people and "trained" seals is that brilliant people get to be the trainer, and they get the fish.

That's how your child becomes brilliant. By you, the trainer, eliciting natural brilliant behaviors from your child that your child is already fully capable of. That's easy because it's all natural. Right now, you're the trainer. Your kid will grow up to become both trainer and seal. I hope your kid likes fish.

IF IT'S NATURAL, WHY DON'T KIDS NATURALLY DO IT?

Very good question. In the beginning, they do. Then us adults mess it up. In the beginning, kids learn everything we throw at them (and some that we try to hide from them) at breakneck speed. Then we decide they need to be educated, and we throw every bit of what made them great learners right out the window. Most of what makes them intelligent goes right into the dumper as well. There's lots more on this in chapters 3 and 4.

My contention is that your child is already capable of brilliance. Your child was born with a tremendously powerful brain and therefore tremendous potential. As I said, the problem is that we squander it. This is great news that should make you jump up and down in your seat a little. Your child has got this. There's nothing to buy, no weird methods needed, nothing time consuming, and nothing that is going to be drudgery for you or your child (it's actually fun). Barring psychological and physiological abnormalities (which need to be addressed by medical and psychology professionals right now) you're all set.

A LITTLE REPETITION

I've got to repeat this to ensure that I'm very clear. Your child already has a brilliant mind. Your child has a brain that is enormously powerful even if your child did not win the genius lottery. Your child is a learning and thinking machine. The problem is that our accepted idea of what learning should be, figuratively beats that potential into the ground like Chuck Norris on a bad guy in the final fight scene. All that's necessary for your child to live a lifetime of brilliance is to retain and build upon the abilities that come with birth. And a couple of very minor tweaks to make it really pay off.

YEAH, SOME KIDS DO HAVE ADVANTAGES...

I hear you. Some children have undeniable genetic advantages. Some have socioeconomic advantages. Your child might jump straight to outright disadvantages. So what? Really, so what? I'm not belittling or dismissing the problems you or your child may be experiencing. I get it. My childhood was no picnic. I had the quintessential evil stepfather who made life terrifying, I was sick, small, and severely bullied throughout school, and we certainly were not in the money. I know the struggles. I'm just not willing to give in or give up on you or your child without a fight. The alternative is to give in to disadvantages and labels and to let your child stay right where others wish.

Keep these things in mind. Labels are often wrong; children rise to your expectations; bad times and bad situations don't always last forever, and most importantly, humans often exceed expectations and even genetic programming. Start from where you are, aim high, grab every opportunity for help you can find, and play the hand you've been dealt, keeping in mind that it's not always the best hand that wins. Often, it's the best player who wins. You can't start any earlier than now, and you can't start ahead of where you are now. But you can start.

What's the worst that could happen? Your child might just reach his or her full potential and it turns out to be short of what you aimed for. But then there your child is, at his or her full potential.

OF COURSE, IT'S MORE COMPLICATED THAN THAT

I know, us humans are a complicated lot. We can mess up anything. Intelligence and learning are not exceptions. Every child is different. Every child's circumstances are different. Every child's goals are different. Many children battle difficulties within and without. But there is tremendous power in the basics and the early years are the time to make the most of them no matter what.

The early years are also the time that it's easiest for you to have a positive impact on your child's intelligence. These are the formative years. You have your child's attention more than you ever will. Your child trusts, and believes in you, more than ever. Use that influence to build the foundation that will support your child for a lifetime of learning and brilliance.

WHAT'S COMING IN THE FOLLOWING CHAPTERS

Chapters 3 through 5 will give you the background needed to understand your child's brilliance. Yeah, the kind of boring stuff. Chapters 6 through 12 are all about how to make it happen. What do you know? Brainpower is easy after all.

3

BRILLIANCE AND INTELLIGENCE

So terribly misunderstood.

BRILLIANT PEOPLE LEARN FASTER, SOLVE problems quicker and easier, seem to magically know what's going on and what to do, and they are exceptionally knowledgeable. Most importantly, it all seems easy for them. That's because it is.

There's nothing weird about being brilliant. Quite the opposite. Being brilliant is what you and your child were designed for. Letting your grey matter atrophy on dumbed-down school, video games, and cat videos is the unnatural state.

Brilliance values intelligence over knowledge.

WHY BRILLIANT?

You're probably wondering why I don't use a word like genius, or intelligent, or gifted, or knowledgeable, or maybe even educated. That's because those words have very narrow meanings. Brilliant is all of those things and more. In the common vernacular, brilliant would mean "really smart."

DON'T WORRY

Right now, you may be worrying that I'm going to help you turn your child into some sort of a mental misfit. Not at all. Unless you consider being a fast-thinking, common sense person who learns with ease a misfit. Okay, I guess you might have a point. Yes, your child will be the exception in a crowd of mental underachievers, but that's a good thing! Just know right now that your child is already capable of brilliance. You're probably going to get tired of me saying that, but it is so vitally important that I'll be repeating it often.

WHAT MAKES YOU THINK MY KID IS BRILLIANT?

Your child has a brain just like everyone else. As I said earlier, barring psychological or physiological abnormalities that brain can do anything anyone else's brain can do. It's not like comparing cars by saying that they all have wheels and an engine. If we use the car analogy, we would have to say that everyone has a multi-million-dollar supercar. The only difference is whether we use it to its full potential, use it simply as a grocery-getter, or leave it in the garage gathering dust and rusting away.

So, is your child using his or her brain to its full capability now? Nope. Almost no one does. We're not even capable of operating at full capacity continuously. It's not even necessary. But we do need your child to function well above the level that is generally accepted as typical. Luckily, that's an easy goal and not the least bit out of the realm of possibility. That's partly because the bar has been set very low and partly because it's just plain easy.

SO, HOW MUCH OF OUR BRAIN ARE WE USING?

There's a huge debate among scientists and researchers about our brain usage, but there's pretty much a consensus that we can all use much more than we do. Many of us don't use much at all. Sorry, but it's true. In my opinion, we're using less and less. There's also a lot of debate about just what, or how much, you can do about it. Let's see if we can clear all that up a bit.

DO WE USE ONLY 10% OF OUR BRAIN?

It used to be common for people in the brain research business to say that we use only 10% of our brain's capability. You've probably heard that a thousand times. In the past few years, people in the business of brain research have begun to loudly challenge that theory. They very accurately state that, through the use of brain scans, they can see that we all utilize every part of our brain regardless of our level of smarts. They say therefore the 10% brain usage statement is bunk. They point out that no-one uses just 10% of their brain as if that means some tiny corner hidden behind one of your ears. These experts are misstating the 10% theory. They've changed it from its original meaning.

Of course, we all use every part of our brain. The point was, and still is, that very few of us use more than a fraction of our brain's capability, not real estate. That's a huge difference. It also may not be 10%. It may be 15%, 25%, or maybe even 50% (I doubt the 50% number). The fact is that there is a lot of potential left on the table no matter how much you are currently using. Let's say, just for discussion, the 10% brain capability usage estimate is correct. And I'm a super genius who uses a whopping 25% of my brain's capability. That's great. But it also means there is 75% left that your child can use to leave me in the intellectual dust. So, I'm nothing special at all at 25%.

Do you get where I'm going here? Ignore the whining about the 10% usage debate and just know that there is huge, usable brain potential right there in your little one's head that is just waiting to light up and get to work. Small improvements can yield huge results. It really doesn't take much.

If you don't believe there is unused potential in everyone's brain, take a look around you. Consider the fact that anyone can become an expert in any field with around five years of intense study. Are any of your friends, family, or coworkers leaving that potential on the table? Yeah, I thought so.

You should know right now that your child can be brilliant without even coming close to using the brain's full potential. That makes it sound easier, doesn't it?

SCIENCE FIGHT!

There is also much disagreement about whether or not intelligence can be increased and if intelligence is determined more by nature (what you're born with), or nurture (your environment). The nature crowd argues that you're born with smarts, or you're not. Give up now and go back to watching cat videos. The nurture crowd believes your environment and interactions with others plays a large part in the development of your intelligence. Dispense with the cat videos, grab a good book, and talk about it with a smart friend.

HOW ABOUT AN ANALOGY?

I own a set of golf clubs, and I play a little golf. Tiger Woods also owns golf clubs and has been known to smack the little white ball around. He's got arms and legs. I have arms and legs. Still, there are some serious differences in how we perform on the links.

Is that because he was born with an innate ability to swing a golf club at genius level? Maybe, but I don't think so. Tiger keeps himself in shape, but I don't think he's a physical phenom. More on that later. In Tiger's case, the man worked from childhood to develop his skills. Heck, at his peak he still worked tirelessly adjusting his swing and every other aspect of his game. Tiger stinking knows golf. He has learned, developed, and refined every aspect of golfing both mentally and physically to an extremely high level. However, had he never been taught, from that young age, how to use his mind and body for golf he might play no better than I do (okay, maybe not that bad).

I have everything needed to be a great golfer just like Tiger. Yet, he's a super golfer, and I'm decidedly not. That's why I keep saying, "Play the hand you're dealt and play to win. And it's not always the best hand that wins. Often, it's how that hand is played."

When it comes to brainpower, performance is tremendously dependent on how well you've learned to use what you've got. So, for brilliance, I fall very firmly on the nurture side. Can your child become brilliant? Ya darn skippy. That's because brilliance is much more than just brain cells. Brilliance is very much the result of learning the skills of intelligence.

As for the nature stance. Sure, genetics can play a role in mental or physical performance. That is easily evident in athletic performance (think powerlifter vs. marathoner). It's much more difficult to ascertain for mental performance though. I really don't care. If your child is one of those rare geniuses that's great. If your child isn't, that's great too. Because like me being born with what I need to play Tiger Woods level golf, your child was born with everything necessary to be brilliant. It's all about putting it to use. I don't think Tiger had any huge physical advantages. He just learned the basics very early, he made them a natural part of him by learning to the point of subconscious proficiency.

Myth-busting time.
Let's put this to bed. Developing brainpower is not like building muscle. That analogy doesn't hold water. See BRAIN-BOOSTING GAMES on page 30.

Before we go any farther. Is it necessary to play as well as Tiger to be considered a brilliant golfer? No again. There are brilliant golfers working at your office, at your local club, and flipping burgers at the golden M diner. Being a brilliant golfer means demonstrating outstanding golfing abilities. Is it necessary to be a genius to be brilliant? No again (no is trending).

ONE MORE LOOK AT NATURE VS. NURTURE

If a child is figuratively raised by wolves (I'm sure you know a few), never being taught basic knowledge and skills that child would be unable to do simple math, speak somewhat grammatically correct, would be ignorant of common skills, and would often be socially inappropriate. That child would be thought of as unintelligent. Let's consider a pair of twins.

Twin one – She is raised in a mentally neglectful environment where she spends her days with very little human interaction. She is provided very little challenging or positive mental stimulation. Everything is done for her, so she learns how to do nothing herself. It doesn't help that she has someone there to remind her often, if only with a look of disdain, that she will never amount to anything of value.

Twin two - The second child is raised in an environment that provides copious stimulating human contact, she's taught basic thinking skills, she gets to fail and succeed with tender guidance, she is provided constant opportunities for being creative, she receives an education that provides the knowledge necessary to inform and inspire her, and she's afforded a small measure of mindless entertainment to balance the day. It helps that there is always someone there to affirm her accomplishments and to lovingly, but honestly, address her failures.

Now try to tell me that environment isn't going to play a part in how "smart" these two children will be. Their genetic potential will be unchanged, but big deal. Nature has already had its butt kicked by their environment.

BUT MY KID IS JUST NOT INTELLIGENT

Really? Okay, so your kid eats dirt and sticks things in his nose. I know a very successful attorney who ate crickets when he was a kid. Anyway, you're convinced that your child isn't intelligent. I'm not, but you are. What to do? Kick that thought out of your head right now! That's what. Your child may think differently than you expect. Your child may not learn quickly. Your child may have zero interest in learning (a clear sign of being a normal kid). But your child still has a brain.

Can you think of something that your child is interested in? Ask your kid about it. Ask for the details. Don't judge. Sure, it's a useless pursuit, but I bet your child will tell you details about whatever it is that will astound you. Your kid is intelligent but just hasn't become interested in applying that intelligence to what you expect or want. And, if you're starting late, your child isn't conditioned to think (there's much more on that in chapter 6).

Ignore the labels, ignore the grades, ignore your feelings, and make the absolute most of what your child has. What other choice do you have? Give up on your child? Heck no.

Humans have a habit of exceeding expectations and rendering labels meaningless. Kids are the greatest at this because it's so early in the game for them. All they need is for you to guide them, believe in them, and not give up on them. Oh, and you need to teach them to use their intelligence. That's covered in chapters 6 through 12.

It's a good news, bad news situation.

Being close to your child every day gives you the opportunity to teach, influence, and guide. It also lets you see every dumb thing the kid does. Us humans tend to gravitate to the negative, especially when we're the ones who have to clean up the mess. Do your best to be objective so you can see the good and the improvements. Accept the bad as a kid being a kid just making discoveries. And ignore those who don't understand your child as well as you do.

THE QUICK AND DIRTY TRUTH ABOUT IQ AND IQ TESTS

Speaking of labels... The goal of an IQ test is to test one's intelligence (reasoning ability) independent of knowledge. In other words, an IQ test wants to assess how smart you are, not what you know. Of course, that's impossible because you need to know something in order to be tested.

Math and vocabulary along with a general knowledge of social interactions and all sorts of other information are always part of even the best-designed IQ tests. Scoring does consider the test taker's age in an effort to offset the knowledge variable to some extent. Experts design the tests and then other experts come behind them to explain why the test is rubbish. The only consensus is that IQ is certainly not everything when evaluating your child's intelligence and potential. It can be a small part of the big picture but never everything.

DIDN'T GET THE SCORE YOU WANTED?

IQ tests vary widely. If your child didn't get the score you wanted on one test, just try another. The methods and question types employed by the tests can be drastically different. It's luck of the draw, but hopefully, you'll encounter one that suits your child better. You can also train for it (not so much for very young children). Yup, there are tons of books (and some websites) on how to score better on IQ tests. They present examples of the types of questions you can expect, and then they explain the most effective strategies for answering them. A few years ago, I read one of those books and then scored a 181 on an IQ test. I absolutely do not have a 181 IQ. I just had lots of inside information and quite a bit of practice under my belt. A smarter, but less prepared person, would easily score lower but their score would be much more accurate and meaningful.

Warning!
If you are inclined to have your child practice for an IQ test, be careful. I have seen very few IQ test practice books or websites that are legitimate. Be wary of wasting your time, money, and effort. Go for practice materials that are produced by the test's creator or publisher whether in print or online.

IQ test practice does not make your kid smarter.
Practice does help your child become more adept at answering IQ test type questions. Your kid may develop strategies and thought

processes applicable to those types of questions. There's also tremendous benefit in just becoming familiar with IQ test type questions and the time management requirements of taking an IQ test. The higher score that may result though is not indicative of higher intelligence. It's really best to skip practice entirely.

IQ TESTING CAN HAVE A POSITIVE OR A NEGATIVE EFFECT

Scoring poorly on an IQ test can be devastating, especially for a child. They take labels very seriously. Conversely, scoring very high can give a false sense of superiority that may lead to a degree of apathy. In high school, I was constantly told I was stupid because of my poor grades and because I thought very differently than my teachers. So, when I scored very high on a Mensa* test just a few years out of high school, it was a very positive experience (Mensa* is a club that requires an IQ in the top 2% of the general populace for membership). I hesitate to think how I would have responded if I had the misfortune of encountering a test on which I would have scored poorly. The point is that I would have been the same person with the same intelligence level either way. So is your child.

FULL DISCLOSURE

Mensa actually administered two tests the day I tried out. I exceeded Mensa's* requirements on one by scoring into the top 1% but I fell 1% short on the other.*

WHAT ABOUT MY CHILD'S IQ RESULTS?

There's a lot to think about when it comes to your child's IQ test results. The most important thing to consider is that you know your child better than anyone else. As long as you're not in denial

*Mensa is a registered trademark of American Mensa, Ltd.

about a real problem, you are the most qualified person to assess the validity of the test results.

An exceptionally low IQ score does merit further scrutiny by highly qualified psychology professionals. Yeah, plural. Never trust the final say to a single individual. A second and third opinion is always a good idea. Maybe even a fourth.

Keep in mind that a very low IQ score can be indicative of many things. Difficulties caused by poor reading skills, dyslexia, depression, anxiety, fear of labeling, and many other factors can easily result in a low score. Don't expect your child to tell you either. They're notorious for keeping important information like that to themselves.

"EXPERTS" LOVE LABELS

Don't let an "expert" label your child just because your child presents an opportunity for the expert to play with their toys. Don't get me wrong. Very often experts can save the day for your child. Often, they are the only ones who have the answers you need. I just want you to be heavily involved and to always consider everything that you see about your child that the expert does not see. That label they put on your child will be seen by many who will not understand it as well as you or the expert who put it there. That includes your child so be very careful and stay as informed and as involved as you possibly can.

HAVE A TALK WITH YOUR CHILD

If your child is older, the two of you need to have a talk about intelligence. Ask your child, "Who decides if you're intelligent? Your friends? Your grandparents? Your teachers? Your spelling test? Your EOGs (end of grade tests)?" No! None of the above.

Say to your child, "You were born intelligent, you've got this." Go on to say, "The fact that you have everything necessary to be intelligent has decided this. Sure, you may be getting poor grades, kids may be calling you dumb, and your teacher may not see your intelligence but that is their ignorance on display. I know it's very hard to believe when everyone around you is telling you otherwise, but you must. You display it in so many ways that it is not up for discussion." Then list some of the ways that you've committed to memory before you started this conversation.

Those ways that you've noted can be anything from worthwhile academic achievements to worthless, time-wasting interests. It doesn't matter for this purpose. Your goal is to build your child's belief in his or her abilities. You can channel and guide those intellectual powers to more desirable pursuits later. For now, point out how your child memorizes sports stats, your child's vast knowledge of skateboarding and skateboards, the incredible collection of song lyrics that are memorized, the foreign language of texting that has been mastered, etc. I think you get the idea. Hopefully, this is convincing you as well. The goal here is to get your kid on board and believing.

UNDERSTANDING INTELLIGENCE

This is fundamental to understanding everything else in this book. Intelligence is a basic and vital component of brilliance. Unfortunately, intelligence is very misunderstood. Let's clear some of this up by looking at a few comparisons.

Educated vs. Intelligent

This is the biggie. Education has nothing whatsoever to do with intelligence. You can be very highly educated and not be able to think your way out of a wet paper bag. Conversely, you can be an octogenarian with no more than a fourth-grade education and still be highly intelligent. Education simply means that you have received instruction. It doesn't mean that you can effectively utilize what you've been taught. Intelligence is the ability to act upon, utilize, acquire, and create with information.

Knowledge vs. Intelligence

You can know a whole lot and still be dumb as a stump. As Einstein said, "Knowledge has no bearing on intelligence." Knowledge is just information. That can come in handy if you make your living as a game show contestant. Intelligence is the ability to understand, utilize, and create with knowledge.

Ignorance vs. Stupidity

This one gets under my skin. Ignorance is a word that gets thrown around a lot errantly. Likewise, the word stupid gets slapped on people who don't deserve it. Ignorance is just the absence of knowledge. It simply means that you do not know something. We're all ignorant about countless subjects. There is no shame in ignorance unless it is by choice or the result of intellectual apathy. Stupidity is acting unintelligently. That's usually by choice or through apathy. It's not the absence of a capacity for intelligence which would indicate a malady that is out of that person's control. Stupidity is a choice and therefore is problematic. It means that you do things errantly or remain ignorant by choice. Yes, that is stupid.

!!! NEVER !!!

Some kids have cognitive deficits due to medical or psychological conditions that are beyond their control. Yes, they cannot display intelligence at the level of kids who do not suffer from those afflictions. But that is NOT stupidity, and I detest and challenge anyone who labels them so. If those children are performing to the best of their ability and doing the best they can, I call that brilliant. Just because you can't do a hundred pushups, doesn't mean you don't have strength.

A Student vs. C Student

This can get a little confusing. Either of these can be brilliant and either of them can be... well... not brilliant. A students can reach this achievement through memorization or by being brilliant. C students can be lots of things. They can be less than outstanding intellectually but trying hard, or they can be brilliant but bored, disinterested, overloaded, disadvantaged, or otherwise impaired. Discerning the difference requires knowing the kid and the kid's situation. Never take school grades, good or bad, at face value. Unfortunately, that's what most of our society does.

Brilliant vs. Everything Else

Brilliance encompasses everything that you associate with intelligence and being "smart." Being brilliant just means that you are very practically intelligent. Brilliant people acquire and utilize information with less effort. Their thinking, while not perfect, is reliable and innovative. Brilliant people typically function intelligently in most situations.

NONE OF MY BUSINESS

I'm not going to tell you or your child what to think. I'm just going to show you how to ensure that your child's intelligence is operating at its full potential for whatever purpose you and your child deem appropriate. That includes being successful in their educational pursuits whether they are in public school, private school, or in homeschool. For full disclosure, I must tell you that I greatly favor homeschool.

THE OBLIGATORY RIGHT-BRAIN, LEFT-BRAIN DISCUSSION

Ugh. Yes, it's true that the two hemispheres of the human brain tend to handle different aspects of thinking. But this right-brain (creative), left-brain (logical) stuff has gotten far away from what science tells us about how the brain works. In short, forget about it. Your brain does not divide tasks by type and then delegate those tasks to one side of the brain or the other. Your child's entire brain is involved in nearly everything nearly all the time.

Here's how you should think about this. There are logical aspects of thinking, and there are creative aspects of thinking, and your kid needs both. And... here's the biggie... both sides are required, to some extent, for all thinking. Do you know that Leonardo da Vinci's paintings are also mathematical masterpieces of detailed studies in perspective and geometry? I don't mean by accident. He plotted, planned, measured, and calculated in tremendous detail before ever putting down a drop of paint. How about that non-starving artists understand the business side (lots of math) of art as well?

So, what to do? Expose your child to as many types of thinking as possible, preferably through play and experience. Combining creative and logical thinking in problem-solving and creative endeavors is even better (exactly what we're going to do later). The synergetic effect of combining logical and creative thinking cannot be overstated. Have your mathlete learn to play a musical instrument (music is very mathematical) or the like and have your artist study business and high-level math. And don't wait for your child to reach school age. Creativity and logic can be a part of play and teaching for your toddler too (just include logical play and creative play). Along the way, your child will probably gravitate to one or the other. That's when you need to help them understand the importance of the types of thinking that have become of less interest (or sneak them in).

Duck Rescue

I'm reminded of an anecdote I once read in Reader's Digest. A dad recounted a day when he was constructing a fence on his farm. He had first dug several deep holes for fenceposts. His four-year-old son came to him frantically telling him that a duckling had fallen into one of the holes. He was begging his dad to rescue the imperiled duckling. His dad dashed to the scene and reached into the hole to no avail. The hole was too deep. There was no way he could reach the duckling. He tried every way he could to devise a plan to save the duckling, but none of them worked. He finally had to break the news to his son that the poor little duckling was not going to make it. The young boy looked up at his dad and asked, "Why don't you float him out?" Now, the dad had expended a lot of effort, and I'm sure he had thought through all the conventional (and logical) ways to reach the little duckling, but it was the no-limits thinking (creativity and logic) of a child, that saved the day... and a duckling.

BRAIN-BOOSTING GAMES

If you're expecting an IQ boost, don't waste your time and money. Supposed brain-boosting games have been all the rage in the past few years. The premise is that, if you work out your brain by solving increasingly complex puzzles of various types, you'll become smarter, develop a better memory, etc. Unfortunately, that's not how the brain works.

Most of these games have problems similar to the problems with our education system. They break thinking down into separate brain functions and types of thinking. This completely disregards the synergy of how our brains work. It's like trying to teach someone to ride a bike by explaining sitting, handlebar gripping, pedaling, and balance in separate lessons. That bike will rust into dust before the learner ever rides an inch. We can't improve an isolated aspect of intelligence and expect to be generally smarter. It won't work no matter how hard we work on every one of the pieces.

On the other hand, if your child finds brain-boosting games to be fun there's little harm. And your child may develop specific strategies for problem-solving in particular situations. When you develop your own strategy for doing something mentally, you own it. If your kid does this, and it works for your kid, don't try to change it. Of course, you-must-show-your-work teachers will demand it so expect that battle and be ready to tell the teacher to try to keep up.

Many mental math experts attribute their talents to shortcuts they devised as kids. Those shortcuts typically utilize mental imagery as well as logic. Your kid's strange way of doing things can often turn out to be very advantageous.

QUOTING EINSTEIN? THE GUY COULDN'T FIND HIS SHOES.

Yes, Albert Einstein was a bit of an absent-minded genius. But he's still a great example for us (including your kids). Expectations for him were very low when he was young, proving labels don't define you. He was multitalented, including being an accomplished violinist. He was well known for his great sense of humor, making him very human. Most of all, he credited play and imagination for all of his accomplishments. And he had a lot to say about the uselessness of what we call education.

Did you know that Einstein never said much of what you see as quotes on motivational posters and memes?

THE BOTTOM LINE

It is imperative that you understand that newfound super abilities are not the answer. It is not necessary to turn your child into a genius. It's much easier than that. Your child already has a brain that is capable of brilliance.

You must also understand that intelligence is not grades, diplomas, degrees, or facts that can be regurgitated on command. Intelligence is the ability to think. Intelligence is much more important than knowledge.

You must begin now to endeavor to not let your child's natural brilliance be suppressed and destroyed. That may not sound exciting, but it is truly the most important thing that you can do for your child's brilliance. There's much more on this in the following chapter.

Lastly, live a life that teaches your child to think and teaches your child the skills of intelligence. That will set your child up for lifelong brilliance. That's what we will be doing in chapters 6 through 12.

4

THE ENEMIES OF BRILLIANCE

School is where brilliance goes to die.

THE BIGGEST PROBLEM YOUR CHILD FACES IS loss of cognitive ability. I can hear you saying, "But I thought this book is about how my child can become smarter." You're absolutely right. It is extremely important for your child to learn to develop and better utilize intelligence. That's actually the easy part because your child's brain is already capable of brilliance and your child's natural way of thinking and learning are perfectly suited to brilliance.

The problem is that there are tremendous forces that will snuff those abilities like a sumo wrestler sitting on a kitten. The cognitive loss is typically devastatingly tremendous, and the forces that cause that loss are ubiquitous. Even worse is that one of those forces is commonly believed to be a source of intellectual development. For now, understand that it is much easier to protect and preserve your child's brilliance than it is to reclaim it once it's lost to these intelligence stifling beasts.

THIS ISN'T GOING TO SIT WELL WITH MANY OF YOU

That's because, in the following chapters (especially in this one), I'm going to fly right in the face of much of what you've been led to believe. School will not make your child intelligent (that goes for college too); educational toys are mostly worthless, and being bored is good for your child's brain. School is first on the chopping block.

A NOTE TO, AND ABOUT, TEACHERS

Don't read this as an indictment of teachers. If you want to read this as an indictment of our educational system and methods, have at it, because it is. The biggest problem for teachers is that they are required to use methods that are proven failures. Even a great teacher often can persevere only so long under the system's pressure. High school and college taught them using the same teach-for-the-test system that will fail your children. In college, aspiring teachers are taught very little about intelligence or how humans learn. I know there are some teachers out there who fight the system and do it right despite the pressure. That's not easy for them to do and they typically pay a heavy price.
Cheers to them!

ENEMY NUMBER 1

When it comes to intelligence, school is the problem, not the solution. In fact, school is the archenemy of brilliance and intelligence. Yeah, I mean that. I can hear you saying, "But that's where kids go to learn." and "How can that possibly be?" and "But my child gets straight A's!" The way we "educate" our kids is a brain-wasting, inefficient, dumbed-down, mess.

> *"I never let my schooling interfere with my education."*
> – Mark Twain

The core problem is that schools are knowledge-centric rather than intelligence-centric. Brilliance is the exact opposite. Brilliance emphasizes intelligence. Intelligence makes every aspect of learning and knowledge utilization easier. So, why in the name of all that makes any darned sense at all do schools barely even mention intelligence?

Do you remember a single day in school that you were taught how to learn? How to be intelligent? How your mind works? How to use intelligence? Go to all the teachers you can find and ask them to tell you all about how to learn and intelligence or what they were taught about learning and intelligence in college. Bring coffee and a snack to have while they struggle to come up with an answer. It's just something they weren't taught and that they are not charged with. So, don't expect your child's teacher to know anything about intelligence and how kids learn. If they do answer, it will be something along the line of, "Have a clean workspace, two sharp pencils, and a quiet room." Yeah, that's about it. Homeschoolers, many of you are not off the hook either. If your homeschool is just school at home, meaning that you've just brought the school's problems to your house, there's not much difference intelligence wise.

Schools aren't interested in intelligence. It's just not what they do. Schools are in the knowledge business, and they do that only to the extent they're required to in order to meet standards set by a faceless committee. School systems are only interested in what they can replicate across a wide spectrum of students and what they can quantify to document results. They set the bar very low and they consistently fail to reach it. It's teach-for-the-test, teach-for-the-test, real learning be darned. That's why community colleges across the country are forced to provide remedial classes even for recent high school graduates. Very recently, they've begun to add basic classes in math that are below the remedial courses. It's very, very sad.

Our education system has done for intelligence and learning what the fast-food industry has done for fine cuisine.

Schools want to be knowledge factories. They take brilliant, dynamic, active, creative kids and plunk them down in chairs so they can listen to a boring adult drone on and on about this and that so the kid can regurgitate what's been said for a test so they can move on to the next boring topic. Don't forget to toss in a couple of orders to "sit still" and "be quiet" to complete the picture. It's a wonder that kids learn anything. Everything that made your child a fantastic learner is forced to shut down, and adherence to the dumb slow way is rewarded.

"Teaching should be such that what is offered is perceived as a valuable gift and not as a hard duty."
-Albert Einstein

Of course, intelligence is useless without knowledge upon which to act. Knowledge is vitally important. Knowledge, though, is more easily obtained by an intelligent approach with an engaged, intelligent mind. In other words, if you're smart, learning stuff is easier. So, why does school try to pound in knowledge all day with little to no concern for development of intelligence or intelligence utilization skills? It just makes no sense. That is unless the goal is to stuff just enough knowledge in your child's brain to hit that very low bar I mentioned earlier so your child can be shuffled on to the next grade. That is not learning.

Educated Does Not Equal Intelligent

THE DUMB WAY SCHOOLS IMPART KNOWLEDGE

Have you ever noticed that the root word of rote is "rot?" Rote learning is poison to intelligence, but it's the go-to method at schools of nearly every flavor. That includes many homeschools, by the way. Rote learning is the very same method used for teaching parrots to speak. Many parrots are very intelligent (for parrots), but very few of them go on to successful careers.

It's true that repetition is a viable strategy for moving knowledge into long-term memory. Water is good for you too but not by the 55-gallon drum. Do you like having things repeated to you over and over like someone believes you're stupid? Well, your kid doesn't like it either. If you want to engage your child's intelligence, you've got to express a little confidence in them and be patient when they need a do-over.

The school brand of rote learning is nearly void of engagement, it's degrading, and it's nearly terminally boring (ever wonder why your kids tune school out?). Most importantly, it is void of understanding, real challenge, high expectations, and real interaction. Sure, some kids need a little extra repetition, but they still need to be challenged and engaged. Nearly every school falls flat in that department, and brilliance gets squashed when they land.

THE RESULT OF ALL OF THIS

That fabulous brain in your child's head, the one that acquired a language or two in no time, the one that created wonderful stories and works of art leaves school at age eighteen as an atrophied, paint-by-numbers shadow of what it could have been. Heck, by the end of the first year, the damage is pretty much done. Sure, your kid will have a diploma but at a terrible cost.

BUT MY KID'S SCHOOL...

It's about this time that the response is usually, "But my child's school is wonderful." No, it's not. Your child's school may have some great teachers, but the teaching methods and the system are proven failures. Sure, some kids thrive in school, but they're the exceptions, not the rule, and it's because those kids are either brilliant, very tolerant, highly motivated, or all of the above. I want your child to be one of those exceptions, the brilliant one.

"BUT MY KID IS A STRAIGHT-A STUDENT"

Yes, even your A student is being short-changed. Way back in 1981, at the age of 21, I was working at Western Electric as an electronics technician. I was helping many of the older employees who were having difficulty with advancement classes Western Electric was providing. My supervisor at the time knew I was having great success teaching those reluctant learners. He approached me for help with one of his daughters. One of his daughters was a straight-A student while the other was a solid C student. He said, "I have to send my C student out to bring my A student in from the rain."

He wasn't being unkind. He was just succinctly telling me that he recognized that while his A student was obviously scoring great grades, she wasn't making the most of her intelligence. It was around that time that I began saying, "I will take a well-adjusted, common sense C student over a memorizing A student any day of the week." Of course, a well-adjusted, common sense A student would be all the better. I now happen to have a couple of those myself.

School was failing his A student. She was developing a false sense of accomplishment, and school was bolstering that constantly by rewarding her performance. Don't just read past that. This is one of the most tragic results of our school system. Not only are our kids not taught how to use their intelligence, but they're also rewarded for achieving pitiful benchmarks. What better way is there to condition your child to underachieve?

Regurgitating information from a study sheet, memorizing a word list, and remembering where to find answers in an open-book test all have very little correlation with the development of intelligence or learning to any useful measure.

YOUR CHILD CAN BE IN SCHOOL AND STILL BE BRILLIANT

Your child can keep, and increase his or her brilliance, even while in school. School will be much easier for them. That's my goal, to teach you how to ensure that your child keeps and even increases the innate brilliance that comes with birth. However, keeping your child brilliant while in school is kind of like keeping a boat afloat that has a few holes in it. While you are bailing water and patching holes, school is going to be constantly poking new holes and screaming that you're the one sinking the boat.

Early in my son's second-grade year, I was called in for a meeting with his teacher because he was doing his math differently than she expected. Never mind that his worst grade was a perfect score. I took a seat in front of her desk, and my son went to a back corner of the room where there were toys to amuse him. After listening to her tell me about his math difficulties, I asked her to do something for me. I had her place a calculator in front of her. I would call out mathematical problems to my son. She was to follow along. I called out a series of ten or so calculations like 355 plus 472, divide that by 8, add 5,637, multiply that by 6, subtract 4688, and so on. She had difficulty keeping up. When I stopped my son had the correct final answer (to two decimal places). He also never even looked up from his playing. Her immediate response was to ask me to meet with the high school math teacher so he could make me understand how I was messing up my kid. I said, "No thanks." Imagine if she had responded by asking me how I taught him to do that. She could have asked me to help her other students to learn. Nope. That didn't fit her mold, not the way we do things, blah, blah, blah. Very sad.

THE BOTTOM LINE

We need to ensure that your child succeeds in school and maintains the brilliance that was there before school began its assault. Our society has made success in school a necessity. School (private, public, or homeschool) is the only route to the hall-pass (diploma) needed to get into college where the teaching model is even worse, much worse. So, it is imperative that your child performs well in school. Being brilliant will make that happen much more easily.

The only downside to having a brilliant kid in a dumbed-down school is that you're going to have to keep your child challenged. You might think that advanced and gifted classes will be the answer. Nope. While they may help a little, they're basically just more of the same rote rot. School is what it is. To keep your child engaged and challenged you'd do better to focus on other interests such as music, arts, sports, and college classes that actually interest your child. Many elite colleges, like MIT, make some of their classes available online for free. Don't get me wrong. I'm not endorsing all colleges. But those college classes can be great for adding challenge for your high schooler or even your middle school child. Keep your eyes wide open though. Colleges have their own special ways of messing up education.

ENEMY NUMBER 2

Screens. Ugh, I dread getting into this debate, but it must be done. Yeah, I know. Screens provide lots of useful information, kids must learn to use technology, and they keep your kid out of your hair when you're busy. And, of course, there's no way to stop them because screens are everywhere, and obviously, every three-year-old needs a smartphone (insert sarcastic eye roll).

Science has already determined that screen time is literally rewiring children's brains. They're not ready to say if that is definitely a bad thing because their study methods require more time and evidence (as they always do). While we're waiting, we can just go with what we all intuitively know. Games, mindless videos, and the Internet, in general, are like digital meth to a kid. Don't believe me? Just try taking a teenager's phone away. Constant entertainment is not only a massive waste of time but also a destroyer of imagination (the foundation of intelligence). "How?" you ask. By letting your child live someone else's imagination instead of using their own. Dependence on technology for basic memory, calculation, and decision-making leads to intelligence and intelligence skill atrophy. Digital socialization is dangerous and often fraudulent. And the instant gratification that the Internet offers does nothing good for focus, attention span, and the ability to delay gratification. More on all of those in the following chapters.

Sure, mobile devices and computers are a necessary part of life. And your child needs to become a proficient user. But that doesn't mean your kid should be staring at one from sunup to sundown either. My kids didn't get cell phones until age 16. My son was a certified C++ programmer at 15 and was writing IOS apps at age 14 (the developer app has a simulator). Not having a smartphone did not impair his ability to utilize technology. You don't need to worry that not getting a smartphone at age 2 will cause your kid to fall behind.

If your child is very young, go with zero screen time. If your child is very young and has already started, wean them off. If your child is older, you can try weaning off, but it's a longshot. Really, for older kids, you may need to seek professional help breaking the addiction. It's going to be a tough job. Just taking the device away and punishing will be counterproductive at best. Again, go with the professional help option.

GUESS WHO ELSE DITCHED SCREENS FOR THEIR KIDS

Steve Jobs. Yup, Mr. Screenerific himself. He's not the only techno wonder-person to do so. Here are a few quotes from a New York Times article by Nick Bilton dated Sept. 10, 2014.

Recounting a conversation with Jobs in 2010:
"'So, your kids must love the iPad?' I asked Mr. Jobs, trying to change the subject. The company's first tablet was just hitting the shelves. 'They haven't used it,' he told me. 'We limit how much technology our kids use at home'" (Bilton).

Quoting some other tech giants:
"'Chris Anderson, the former editor of Wired and now chief executive of 3D Robotics, a drone maker, has instituted time limits and parental controls on every device in his home. 'My kids accuse me and my wife of being fascists and overly concerned about tech, and they say that none of their friends have the same rules,' he said of his five children, 6 to 17. 'That's because we have seen the dangers of technology firsthand. I've seen it in myself, I don't want to see that happen to my kids.'" (Bilton).

"Alex Constantinople, the chief executive of the OutCast Agency, a tech-focused communications and marketing firm, said her youngest son, who is 5, is never allowed to use gadgets during the week, and her older children, 10 to 13, are allowed only 30 minutes a day on school nights." (Bilton).

"'We have a strict no screen time during the week rule for our kids,' said Lesley Gold, founder and chief executive of the SutherlandGold Group, a tech media relations and analytics company. 'But you have to make allowances as they get older and need a computer for school.'" (Bilton).

The article goes on to debate consumption vs. creativity on devices as well as the wisdom of all-out tech bans and how that may backfire. Regardless, I believe it is safe to say that these movers and shakers in the belly of the tech beast vividly see the potential dark side of letting kids have screen devices too much and too early.

JUST ME BEING REPETITIVE TO DRIVE HOME A POINT

Imagination is the fuel that powers intelligence. Video games, music videos, etc. handle the imagination work while your child passively watches. It's like sitting on the sofa shoving in junk food while watching someone on TV working out.

Actually, it's worse. At least you'll eventually get up off the sofa and use enough muscle power to walk back to the fridge. A screen-addicted kid will rely on that screen for nearly everything. Stop it and stop it NOW!

"But that's were my kid finds inspiration," and "Kids learn hand-eye coordination and problem-solving skills by playing video games." If these are your arguments, reach up and slap yourself across the face a few times. Then grab your lapel and give a few hard shakes too. Snap out of it!

Never use screens as a babysitter. Never!

The biggest problem here is that you're going to get the "everybody else has one" argument. That's why you need to never start in the first place. I did it with ease. I created a normal that didn't include screens and video games. It just wasn't what we did. I never forbade my kids from having one, and they never wanted one. In fact, my kids would often talk about how "dumb" it was to sit and stare at a screen or video game. It was the same for TV (we call it the idiot box).

We did own a Wii* on which only sports were played (the kind where you have to actually stand up and move). We never left it set up, so it required extra effort to get it going. It was primarily there for rainy days. They played it from time to time for up to an hour, but that was it. They haven't touched it since they were around twelve years old.

And yes, my young kids did not have mobile phones, social media accounts, or any other useless tripe, and they never wanted it. Right now, you're probably thinking that they're computer illiterate. As I said earlier, my son was certified as an industry level C++ programmer at age 15 and he was entirely self-taught. My daughter was never interested in computers. At 14, she was using the computer quite a bit, but it was to read about her favorite interests which were divided between quantum physics and crotchet (no, I'm not making that up).

*Wii is a registered trademark of Nintendo of America Inc.

Any harm in the occasional video game?

Heck no. Well, that is if your child does not have a predisposition to addictive behavior. Video games are designed to maintain your interest so they can keep you playing and wanting more. They're kind of an interactive soap opera for kids (and adults). In short, it's very easy to become addicted. Be very careful.

THE BOTTOM LINE

Develop, nurture, and build upon your child's brilliance as much as possible before the school monster comes into the picture. Ensure that your child develops thinking as a habit. You will learn about that in chapter 6.

Don't expect school to develop your child's intelligence. Instead, view school as the enemy of intelligence. It's like the old "*keep your friends close, but keep your enemies closer*" adage. Help your child give school what they want but never accept that as enough. Find every way possible to help your child expand his or her intelligence through other intelligence expanding pursuits.

If you can homeschool, do it. Be careful to not just bring school home. Let your kids learn the way they did as tots with movement, play, fun, interaction, and hands-on experience. Guide, and teach appropriate social norms but don't stifle brilliant thinking and don't make learning drudgery.

Keep your young kids away from screens. Heck, keep older kids away from screens while you're at it. If they do use screens, limit it to the fundamental operation of the device and anything that enables them to use their creativity instead of mindlessly watching someone else's creations.

5

IMAGINATION

It's not magic or weird, it's intelligence.

OH NO! THIS GUY'S GOING TO GO START talking about imagination and a bunch of weird metaphysical junk. He's going to have my kid sitting in the lotus position chanting mantras and gargling green tea. Nope. It's nothing like that. Imagination is simply the ability to create images and ideas in your mind. It's the foundation of all human intelligence. Your child can't be brilliant without imagination.

> *"When I examine myself and my methods of thought, I come close to the conclusion that the gift of imagination has meant more to me than my talent for absorbing absolute knowledge."*
> – Albert Einstein

You imagine constantly all day, and I bet very few of you gargle green tea, and some of you can't even get into the lotus position. Don't believe me? Not the green tea gargling part, the imagination part. I'll prove it to you. Then I'll do you one better. I'll prove that the greatest minds in history proactively used imagination.

Have you ever thought about how your living room would look if you moved your sofa? Have you ever woke up and wondered, "Where are my slippers?" and envisioned where they might be? Have you ever stared at something that's broken and thought of ways to fix it? Yup, you've used your imagination.

BIG MISTAKES

Many people think of imagination only for artistic endeavors like music, writing, poetry, or humor. Others regard imagination as what the mind does when wasting its time. Well, those are huge mistakes, and they're just plain wrong. Imagination is everything when it comes to intelligence and brilliance. Without imagination, you can forget about problem-solving, socializing, learning, memory, or virtually anything else you would like to do with your intellect. Imagination is not whimsy, it's a powerful and practical mental ability that is absolutely essential to brilliance.

"Imagination is more important than knowledge. Knowledge is limited. Imagination encircles the world."
– Albert Einstein

IMAGINATION COMES FIRST

Nothing gets created unless someone sees it in their mind first. I will go so far as to say that every great discovery (as well as every very small discovery) has been the result of imagination. Uh oh. This is typically when the response is, "Hah! I've got you now. Some of the greatest discoveries of all time have been by accident!" Yup, that's true, but realizing the application of what was discovered required imagination. It had to be seen in the mind first. Imagination wins again.

DOES IT COME FROM THE COSMOS?

Heck no. As wild as our imaginations can be (you should see my dreams), the process is practical at its roots. Everything your imagination does is based on information that is in your brain (whether you consciously realize it's there or not). It just happens faster and more creatively than your everyday deliberate thinking does. That's because your conscious mind is not in the way. Conscious thought is very slow and limited. High level thought, that seems like it's from the cosmos, requires imagination.

There is a massive amount of information in your brain that you are completely unaware of at a conscious level. Science tells us that our minds limit what we think of consciously. Otherwise, we literally would be unable to function. Tremendous amounts of data are constantly observed, cataloged and stored but never consciously acted upon. To your subconscious mind, those memory stores are a huge toy box just waiting to be played with. By using imagination proactively, you let your subconscious mind dive into that toy box headfirst like a sugared-up three-year-old.

Imagination is faster because it is primarily image-based. Imagine a #2 pencil. You can see it in your mind instantly. Now, describe it to me in complete detail. For something as simple as a pencil, that's still going to take a whole lot of time as you use thousands of words to describe every minute detail of its shape, size, color, etc. You can easily see how much faster the mind is when imagining in images rather than conscious thoughts and words.

All of the information for the image came right from your memory, not the cosmos. That's true when your imagination creates something entirely new as well. It's all a product of your mind using and building upon your memory stores.

> *"The words or the language, as they are written or spoken, do not seem to play any role in my mechanism of thought."*
> -Albert Einstein

That's true of complex thought as well. Imagination is very dependent on what we've termed the "subconscious" mind. Science really doesn't understand the subconscious mind very well, and some scientists even dispute the concept. But there's no doubt that a lot of our thinking happens apart from our conscious thoughts, and nobody doubts the fact that those processes are faster and more powerful than conscious thought.

OBLIGATORY EINSTEIN STORY

Nearly every book on intelligence and imagination tells the story of Einstein and his inspirational experience at age 16. Here's the extremely quick version: Using vivid daydreaming, at 16 young Einstein imagined running alongside a light beam at the speed of light. The images and conclusions his imagination created did not fit the accepted laws of physics.

Most writers focus on the fact that his subconscious mind created what later proved to be accurate, and new, conclusions. That's wonderful, powerful, and true, but I have a different point to make about this. What Einstein's imagination created in moments, using his imagination and subconscious mind, required years for his conscious mind to prove. Did you get that? The conscious mind is slow and far less capable than the subconscious mind. The conscious mind is still vital for sorting things out and directing the subconscious mind, but you must become convinced that imagination is where your child's brilliance is. And you must foster, love, appreciate, and become comfortable with it in every way possible.

We get it right for a while.

Have you ever noticed that children's books (the good ones) are full of imagination evoking content? Then kids get to school, where imagination is requisite for learning, and they encounter textbooks. Ugh.

This is in no way exclusive to Einstein.

Everyone does this. If you've ever daydreamed about the possibilities of anything, you've done this. Get that deep into your head right now. Einstein was smart, but he was a human being just like you and your child. Researchers tell us that Einstein had some very small differences in his brain. Big whoopie poo. Your child's brain can do everything Einstein's could. Some of those differences (like a higher glial cell count) can be the result of a stimulating environment. You're going to provide your kid one of those, right? Your kid has all the parts. Everyone does. Using imagination this way is normal. Not doing this is abnormal.

EDUCATORS AND THE READ, READ, READ CROWD

Educators who are so fond of the "well rounded" education extol the near requisite reading of copious quantities of literature both classic and contemporary. Well, you wouldn't have a single one of those books without imagination. They are all products of imagination, even the non-fiction ones. The reader's imagination is integral to the experience as well. Reading those books would be little more than passive observation of ink on paper if the words did not evoke images, feelings, and thoughts that are the result of imagination. Not engaging imagination when reading reduces comprehension as well as retention. More importantly, it negates the progression of thought that would occur in the reader's mind as imagination interplays the ideas read with the ideas and information already in the reader's mind.

Bonus Tip!

Want to help your child read faster? Let your kid trace the lines with their finger or a guide. Retracing and inefficient eye movement are major factors in reading speed. Just using a guide to consistently keep your place can up reading speed tremendously. Not losing your place helps with concentration and comprehension as well as just making it easier to stay on topic. You might want to have a defibrillator handy for your kid's teacher though.

READING WITH IMAGINATION IN MIND

Here are a couple of ideas for getting the most out of imagination when reading with your young child:

Read a descriptive passage aloud. Then invite your child to describe more details of the scene and events. This can even include new events and characters. Heck, you might even drop the book and create an entirely new story. You're not only engaging your child's imagination; you're also helping your child develop language and communication skills.

Both parents, and anyone else involved, must read with your child. You each have different styles and will evoke different responses, images, and ideas. Variety is the spice of imagination.

USING IMAGINATION ON PURPOSE

Brilliance is a combination of using imagination as a natural way of thinking (passively) as well as using imagination on purpose (proactively) as a powerful thinking tool for problem-solving as well as creativity. To be brilliant, imagination is always engaged and operating in every aspect of life and passively operating in the background. This will be covered in detail in chapter 6.

Even though imagination is engaged at all times, we can't continuously operate at our absolute peak. For those times that we need to enlist more brainpower than usual, imagination can be enlisted proactively and deliberately for greater effect.

Using imagination proactively is nothing new. Thomas Edison, Albert Einstein, Salvador Dali, Jack Nicklaus, Dwight Stones, as well as Olympic bobsledders, snowboarders, and figure skaters, are all people who have used imagination on purpose with brilliant results.

The famous inventor Thomas Edison and surrealist artist Salvador Dali each realized that they had their best ideas as they were drifting off to sleep. This is a time when the mind is unencumbered by conscious thought, and imagination runs free. They believed this drifting off to sleep effect to be so powerful for idea creation and problem-solving that they devised ways to use it proactively. You see, they had a problem. If they were to drift off to sleep, they were likely to forget their brilliant ideas, solutions, and creations. So, they each had their own method of waking themselves before drifting off completely. Edison would hold a ball bearing over a metal bucket. Dali would hold a heavy key over a plate. The sound of the dropping ball bearing or key would awaken them so they could record their thoughts.

Great athletes like golfer Jack Nicklaus and high jumper Dwight Stones would watch their every movement, and the results, in their minds repeatedly before ever executing an attempt. Jack Nicklaus would stand over the ball before putting and would watch the intended travel of the ball several times before actually striking the ball. Dwight Stones' head would bob up and down as he repeatedly visualized every step of his approach, and then his head would move abruptly as he watched himself clear the bar. Olympic figure skaters and snowboarders can often be seen acting out their events in their minds before performing. Bobsledders, who often have limited access to their competition venue for practice, run their events in their minds often hundreds of times before ever competing. Our Olympic teams employ the services of sports psychologists. Those sports psychologists use guided imagery (proactive imagination) as a tool to enhance athletes' performance with great success.

The point here is that brilliant, intelligent, successful people proactively use their imagination. These people are not in the habit of wasting their time.

Science has shown us that vividly imagining a physical activity fires the same neural pathways in the brain as when we're actually performing those activities. Vividly imagined activity directly translates to actual performance.

TO MY READERS WHO FIND CONFLICT WITH THEIR RELIGION

Some of you may view imagination negatively based on your religious beliefs. Your religion is, of course, none of my business. I am also not a theologian. But please allow me to give some thoughts to consider. Prayer for an outcome that hasn't happened, or doesn't exist, is impossible without imagination.

That which is being prayed for must be seen in the mind first. The concepts of belief and faith are impossible without imagination as they refer to things that are not tangible. An unseen deity is a foundational belief in most religions and requires imagination to conceptualize. And, in most religions, it is that deity who provided you with the brain in your head which cannot function without imagination. I leave you to draw your own conclusions.

THERE YOU HAVE IT

Imagination is important, and we all use it. Well, we use it a little anyway. Your youngster uses it a lot. That's a big part of why your kid is a veritable learning machine. Imagination is important, useful, and essential to getting through the day. Imagine (see what I did there) if you used it proactively, if you and your child put it to work with purpose and focus. Equally important is having imagination engaged passively during every moment of the day. Imagination is thinking. Thinking enables brilliance.

In the following chapters of this book, you're going to learn easy, fun, practical ways to make imagination a lifelong part of your child's thought processes. Imagination will be on automatic for daily life and ready for focused action when needed.

THE BOTTOM LINE

There are two primary ways to use imagination. Passively and proactively. Proactive use can include problem-solving, creativity, and fun. For your young child, we're most interested in developing passive use as a habit and reserving proactive use for fun. Older kids can utilize proactive imagination for problem-solving and for creative pursuits.

BEFORE WE START PUTTING THIS STUFF TO WORK

A few tips.

RULE NUMBER ONE

Never use any of this as punishment. NEVER! You need your child on your side in this. Never create a negative association with intelligence, learning, school, or anything of the like. If your child is starting at a very young age, this is even more important because the associations will be subconscious. Those subconscious associations are very powerful. Your child can easily carry that negative association for a lifetime while completely unaware of it consciously. Subjective memories are always the most powerful. Make them good ones.

DON'T TELL THE GRANDPARENTS WHAT YOU'RE DOING

Well-meaning grandparents and friends are often your biggest enemies when it comes to your child's brilliance. They're almost always stuck on "doing it the way we've always done it." Since my kids were born, my motto has been, "I will never do something wrong for my children to save the feelings of an adult who can get over it." Only tell those who you know will be supportive. Keep all others out of it.

YOUR APPROACH BY AGE

This is an extremely general guide. Every kid is different. No matter the age, always invite participation and imagination no matter how silly it may seem (especially in the very early years).

Birth to toddler – Stealth mode. Never tell them what you're doing.
K4 through 4th – Stealth mode with a dash of explanation.

It doesn't have to stop in the early years

5th thru 8th – Lots of explanation and lots of guidance (from you).
Teens – Fun, fun, and more fun. Interact, enjoy being corrected by your kid, still guide, and stay as involved as possible.

6

5 DIFFERENT WAYS

The number one key to lifelong brilliance.

THIS IS THE MOST POWERFUL AND EFFECTIVE technique in this book. It's also a little anticlimactic. It's the most powerful because it develops nearly every aspect of your child's brilliance. It's anticlimactic because it is so incredibly simple, and because it is something you probably already do, at least to some extent. But there's much more to this than meets the eye, so stay with me.

I've given this the name *5 Different Ways* but that doesn't mean I believe I have created or discovered something new or unique. I call it that just to simplify the discussion and as an easy way for you to remember what we're going to be doing. There is nothing new about 5 Different Ways. That means, although it is underutilized, it has stood the test of time. Because it is something nearly everyone already does (at least a little), we know that everyone can do it. Nearly everyone does it because it's natural, normal, and effective. That's all great news.

If what you're looking for is a complicated, involved, cutting-edge, secret, breakthrough, miraculous, or headline-making method there are plenty of those around if you want to look for them. The problem is that they're typically either too convoluted and time-consuming to use, or they're worthless bunk. Often, they're all of that. Is that what you really want or need? Heck no. You need something that is easy, doable, and effective that fits comfortably into your daily life and your child's daily life. That's exactly what this is. I'll be happy to wait while you do a little happy dance. Nobody's looking.

5 Different Ways is as intuitive as intelligence development can be. It's based on how we like to interact with children and how they think and learn. The only things that are new and different are that we're going to do it much more than typical, we're going to do it with purpose, and we're not going to stop as your kid gets older like most people do.

THIS IS TRAGIC, AND SO EASILY AVOIDABLE

I see a lot of college students struggle. Heck, in the community college system, where they endeavor to serve everyone regardless of academic record, many of them are even having to repeat remedial classes multiple times. In curriculum courses, the struggle is even greater. They have no clue how to handle the data processing, creativity, and problem-solving required. It's not because their brains are incapable. Sure, a lack of study skills can be a contributory factor, but that's easily corrected. What's difficult to overcome is a lifetime of not thinking.

These kids simply don't have thinking skills. They are not in the habit of utilizing their brain's capabilities. Those skills were neglected early on when the foundation should have been built, and our education system perpetuated, supported, and even rewarded that neglect.

Without that foundation in place, they were never able to develop even rudimentary learning and thinking skills that are beyond easy for their powerful brain. Worse, they were unable to build upon those skills over the course of their young lives so that college, and beyond, would be no more than just another easy learning experience. They started behind, and they stayed there. These kids have lived in a 500-room mansion, but they've never left the broom closet.

Don't dismiss this just because you don't anticipate your child experiencing this level of difficulty. K through 12 is not very demanding. It's been dumbed-down, grading scales have been lowered, and studying for the test is often just memorization. So, breezing through school is not an indicator of reasonable intelligence, and it's definitely not indicative of brilliance. Just like driving, experience is not an indicator of skill. Your child is capable of much more.

What's to follow in this chapter may seem silly or even trivial. But through this silliness, your child is going to develop a superior ability (compared to typical) to manipulate and work with data mentally. That improves working memory, creativity, problem-solving ability, awareness, reasoning, communication skills, and general intelligence. Building this foundation now will give your child a tremendous head start and a seriously strong foundation to build upon for a lifetime. You will have set your child's baseline mental abilities very high. The development that will come later will be exponentially greater as a result. Continuing that development is why you must continue 5 Different Ways when others would have abandoned it in favor of "growing up."

THE NUTS AND BOLTS OF THE PROBLEM

We wouldn't be discussing this if there wasn't something going wrong with how things are done now. So, let's talk about it. Most people, when presented with a problem or any situation that requires thought, will stare at the symptoms like a dog at a new bowl. That's where they stop. It's as if they're viewing the world through a straw. They exist almost as stimulus-response beings. And it's not just for the complicated problems. They errantly push on a door that's labeled "pull," and they push again, and again, and maybe a few more times. Their burger lacks pickles, so they go into a rage, oblivious to the consequences. They make poor life choices, they have difficulty learning, they're easy targets for scammers and manipulators, and they're generally unaware of pretty much everything that matters. The world figuratively pokes them, and they respond mindlessly.

They also put the toilet paper on the holder backward, cruise in the passing lane, don't use their signal lights, and hold their phone vertically to video everything. Vertically to video a football game, really?

Some of those examples may sound trivial, but they're nothing of the sort. Everything from our staggering dropout rates to dangerous and deadly fads to generally having difficulty being successful in an everchanging world can be attributed to not thinking and not knowing how to think. Of course, we all make mistakes, but not thinking is more like what my old roommate used to say, "Don't lean into that left hook." By not being in the habit of thinking, they're walking around with their mental chin stuck out just waiting to be intellectually KO'd. We can't blame the kids. They don't know what they don't know. It's up to us adults to teach them to think.

Even sadder is that many people don't want to think. No, I'm not jaded. It's just a fact. I know you see them constantly. They're everywhere. Many people would rather just be along for the ride. They simply don't want to be bothered with thinking, even about the simple stuff. All the while all of these people have the most incredible thinking machine in existence right there in their head just waiting to light up. How can this possibly be? Simple, us humans are path-of-least-resistance beings. We do what's pleasurable, and we avoid what's painful. That's never more true than when we're young.

We start out as brilliant thinking and learning machines full of dynamic energy, enthusiasm, and never-ending curiosity. We roam our new world freely getting the ultimate hands-on (and mouths-on), multi-sensory, fully immersed education possible. Then, as extremely impressionable children, we're yanked out of all that we love (and all that's normal) and are forced into a world that "educates" us by sticking us in a room with a bunch of other kids whom we are forbidden to play with, and one adult who's seemingly only goal in life is to make us sit still and be quiet.

Knowledge and learning are divided into disjointed and disconnected categories of boring, laborious, repetitive tasks that make thinking and learning drudgery. We're even punished if we don't do things the boring slow way (echoes of *"Show your work!"* fill the air). At the same time, we're provided with devices that do our thinking and remembering for us. And we're surrounded by a constant stream of colorful and exciting digital entertainment that leads us away from thinking and creativity.

Who needs that thinking and learning junk when you can just sit back and enjoy the ride? **"More stimulation, please!"**

Intelligence is like beauty.

The concept of beauty cannot be learned by breaking it down into a list of attributes. No matter how long the list, it will still be just a list. Likewise, intelligence cannot be broken down into segments and categories. Intelligence must be developed with full involvement of mind, senses, and body.

TURN BRILLIANCE ON NOW, AND IT WILL RUN ON AUTOMATIC FOR A LIFETIME

THE BASICS

5 Different Ways is based on play and imagination. How great is that? Fun easy stuff! We already know that imagination is the foundation of all intelligence (see chapter 5). And it's a pretty safe bet that your kid likes to play. You're going to play and twist nearly everything you do with, and say, to your child.

You're no longer going to just do things. Just doing things requires very little thought, after the initial learning phase, and it requires no imagination. Just doing things with no thought develops the habit of not thinking and having a very narrow view of the world. Conversely, creatively twisting, playing, and making things humorous requires thought, a quick wit, and imagination. Doing this constantly, even with mundane tasks, develops the habit of thinking. And not just plain old thinking, creative, imaginative, and innovative thinking that sets your child far apart from the stimulus-response crowd.

5 Different Ways develops thinking as a habit, so your child thinks without thinking about thinking. Your child becomes an inherent thinker.

RIGHT NOW, YOU'RE PROBABLY WONDERING IF YOU'RE BEING PUNKED

Nope. That's the basic premise. But there's more detail needed to understand and make the most of 5 Different Ways, and that's where we're going in this chapter. For now, know that it's simple, it's fun, it's easy, and it is what has fueled some of the greatest thinking throughout history. It's also what will fuel your child's brilliance through school and beyond.

By the way.
The number "5" is ambiguous. It's just a way of saying you need to think in multiple ways. It could easily be more. Sometimes less will suffice.

BABES IN THINKING LAND

Children think constantly. That's one reason it's so important to start now. They're into everything. They want to know about everything. They ask questions constantly. They take things apart, and they mix things that maybe shouldn't be mixed. They touch, smell, look at, and taste everything. They don't understand very much, but they're trying to understand, and experience, everything. Right now, your child wants to think. Because their thinking is cleverly disguised as play, they love it. Don't let that go! We're going to use that to our advantage. We want to make the most of it while they're already in that mode before adults and school stuff it in a duffle bag with a cinder block and drop it in a lake.

Your kid already does this. It's what makes your kid a veritable learning machine. All we're going to do is encourage it, build upon it, and prevent it from being turned off.

To make the most of this valuable time of life, we need to do things on your kid's terms. That's why 5 Different Ways is not an interruption to your child's day (or your day). It's not a lesson to be endured. Tell your kid to think all the time and constantly apply their imagination, and you will accomplish absolutely nothing. Live it and enjoy it, and it will stay with your child for a lifetime (as long as you don't let school beat it into submission).

It's much like learning a language. Native speaking ability is easiest to accomplish when we are very young. We learn through immersion in the language and all the subtle nuances that surround it. More importantly, we learn the language before the frontal lobes of our brains fully develop, which is the second reason it's important to start now. That's because those frontal lobes are all about the details, calculating, and analysis. The frontal lobes are the centers for conscious thought. They're also the nitpicking, detail-oriented part of the brain that interrupts us when we're on a roll and leaves us stammering, hesitating, and messing up what typically goes smoothly. Kids learn language without ever a conscious thought about the details because those frontal lobes are not in the way. They just do it.

Don't be confused. When learning a language, the brain is working extremely hard. Language, and all of its subtle nuances, require tremendous computing power. The difference is that, as a young child, this all happens while the kid is blissfully unaware of it consciously. It all happens in the background and forms memories and habits that fire off effortlessly. The power of this is very evident when adults try to acquire a second language. Those frontal lobes kick into full throttle trying to analyze every aspect of cadence, usage rules, tone, etc., etc., etc. with full conscious involvement. The result is slow and painful. If you had learned that second language as a child, with your conscious mind out of the way, it would have been a piece of cake. Both languages would have flowed easily, fluently, and effortlessly.

What if thinking were that natural and fluent?
Ahh, now we're getting somewhere.

WE'RE CREATURES OF HABIT

Habits developed in our very early years are some of our most deeply rooted habits. This is when a tremendous amount of our "normal" is developed. You're going to get tired of me saying this (maybe you already have), but developing thinking as your child's normal, as a habit, is absolutely the difference between brilliance and, well, not being brilliant.

TO THINK WITHOUT THINKING ABOUT THINKING

Brilliant people see solutions before others even realize there is a problem. They're thinking all the time. Not deliberately, naturally. When confronted with a problem, they've ran multiple scenarios through their mind that involve the entire situation, and surrounding variables, while others are still staring at the symptoms thinking, "Who's going to fix this?" This is one of the defining traits of a brilliant person. Their thinking is on all the time just like their language is on all the time. They effortlessly see and understand what others struggle to grasp. The solutions they dream up in an instant are often far outside the box, and sometimes they're smack in the center of the box if they need to be. Everyone around them looks to them for answers. 5 Different Ways makes all of this happen. It's not just thinking. It's thinking with full imagination engagement.

CONDITIONING, IN A GOOD WAY

5 Different Ways is about conditioning your child to think. It

becomes more than a habit. It becomes a part of your child. Thinking becomes as effortless and natural as breathing. It becomes your child's normal.

5 Different Ways is also a very functional way to use imagination with purpose. Too often we think of imagination as something we pause to take advantage of. Kick that thought out of your head, it's a huge mistake. Those who use imagination on the fly with no consideration are inherently powerful thinkers. Of course, there are times that we enlist the power of imagination deliberately for even greater effect, but that level of intensity is difficult to sustain and is therefore not practical for everyday utilization. 5 Different Ways is about the everyday, walking-around type of imagination that fuels brilliance.

A 5 Different Ways example.

When your car's engine fails, you can take it to two types of mechanics. Mechanic one will stare at the engine for a few moments and then will swap parts semi-randomly until finally stumbling upon the problem. Later, you'll receive a very proud, "I fixed it!" and a bill for the defective part and the good parts that were replaced along with the time and cost of the wasted effort changing the good parts. Mechanic two will observe the symptoms and will immediately begin to mentally run a series of what-if scenarios based on his or her knowledge of the systems involved. The mechanic will consider the very complicated scenarios, their variables, and the results of potential cures in multiple ways in mere seconds. The result will be an efficient repair and a reasonable bill.

Mechanic two used a 5 Different Ways way of thinking, and problem-solving. It's nothing magical or new. It's the way any thinking person solves problems.

HOW IT'S DONE

Remember! You're not going to teach your child any weird rituals, strange techniques, or some other-than-natural way of thinking that can damage, or otherwise impair your child's intellect.

You are simply going to trick your kid into thinking, imagining, and creating with their own mind, in their own way, in their own environment, under your guidance, naturally and normally as a course of going through their day. It's what they already do. You're just going to do it more than typical, and you're going to try to keep doing it in the face of a world that wants to squash it like a bug.

As I eluded to earlier, 5 Different Ways means simply to playfully twist, joke, and change that which you and your child do and encounter throughout the day. The difference is that you're going to do this with the intent of taking thinking farther and father and with an element of logic which we'll get into shortly. You want your child to immediately think of the possibilities and alternatives when they do things, whether new or familiar. That's extremely important. Don't reserve this for just new stuff. To be brilliant, your child must constantly consider, and reconsider, the possibilities surrounding the familiar as well.

It's an all-day thinking and imagination game. You're going to engage your child more than in just simple childish-seeming play, keeping in mind the goal to condition your child to think, and to see things in many different ways. If you're putting shoes on your very young child you might put them on your child's hands, then ears, then you might try to put them on your child's feet backward or upside down, you might even turn your kid upside down and place the soles of the shoes on the bottom of your kid's feet. The possibilities are endless. With an older child you might say, "Put a kid in your shoes." or "Your feet are naked." You might make the shoes talk. The shoes could resist or speak with varying accents. Make it all fun, animated, and exciting. The idea is to do it in many different ways, hence *5 Different Ways*. This is only limited by your, and your child's, imagination.

THERE MUST BE AN ELEMENT OF LOGIC

For 5 Different Ways to be effective, there must always be an element of logic and reality to the twists and changes. While nonsense and outrageousness can certainly evoke an imaginative response, it is not directly contributory to brilliance in the form of being an intelligent thinker and problem solver.

A case could certainly be made that outrageous, nonsensical play can lead to creativity of a high magnitude, but I would argue that the very early years are not the time for that. Reserve that kind of imaginative play for an older child or an adult who already has a firm understanding of societal norms, problem-solving, and logic. The early years are very formative and will have a long-lasting effect on your child's thinking and view of the world. Yes, you should have fun with this, but as in the putting shoes on example above, there must be an element of realism and logic in the play so that it is contributory to effective thinking. Like the fact that the shoes were always destined to end up on your kid.

This doesn't mean that your child isn't going to introduce some concepts and ideas that obviously came from outer space. Resist the temptation to immediately shoot those ideas down. Sometimes there is some logic, and some great thinking, hidden deep in those other-worldly ideas. Other times they're pure nonsense. But these are a kid's ideas. Ask lots of questions and guide but never dismiss those ideas without an attempt to understand them first. Throughout history, brilliance has been disguised as lunacy. Then, sometimes lunacy is just that, lunacy. Your job is a tightrope walk for sure.

LIKE LIVING IN A SITCOM

Life for my kids, when they were growing up, was like living in a sitcom. Heck, it still is to this day. My kids grew up learning that the leaves fly south for the winter (Really, hold a map up. Which way is south?). Rather than turn off lights, we would turn on the dark, and instead of driving our car from place to place, we spun the world beneath us.

My kids would often ask me questions at the dinner table (we ALWAYS eat dinner as a family). Immediately after I would answer, they would look to their mother for a nod or a head shake. Usually, they already knew, but it was tradition.

I still pat them on the head, though. That's because I read on the Internet that it makes kids feel loved and appreciated. I tell them all the time that I don't understand why kids love it so much. It would annoy me. That's nuts, right? Of course, it is. I should just tell my kids I love them. Nope. It would go in one ear and out the other. Patting them on the head makes it an event, something to focus on and laugh about. They can't possibly miss that I intentionally gave them my attention and affirmed how I feel about them.

Won't my kid get tired of my corny jokes?
Since they were old enough to understand, I've given my kids a choice. I can be silly, or I can be mean. I can change

any day of the week. It's up to them. They're 18 and 20
now, and they still choose silly.
Go figure.

AGES

Although this is very much a long-term process, you can begin to see your child's brilliance manifest very quickly. How you see the changes will depend heavily on your child's age when you begin.

If your child is still very young, but has already acquired some language and reasoning skills, you can begin to see changes very rapidly. That's because everything is new, and your child is just beginning to join in on the fun. Your child will love the games, and attention, and will join in quickly and enthusiastically.

The interaction and ideas that will spring from your little one's
mind will be evidence of your child's brilliant thinking, but
your work is far from done because that is not indicative of
solidifying thinking as a habit. That is why you need to keep this
going right into school and even into the high school years.

Beginning while your child is still an infant is optimal, but you will miss out on seeing quick changes. That's because you will be establishing your child's thinking habits so early that it will already be a part of who they are when they acquire language and begin to join in. You miss out on seeing rapid changes, but you've gained tremendously by beginning to shape your child's normal from so very early on.

Older kids that have established routines and who have begun to form their normal for daily life will need a little time to adjust. If you haven't been doing anything similar to 5 Different Ways, your child may be confused and may even resist joining in. Keep it fun, apply zero pressure, and just persist. Watch your child closely to pick up on what works and what doesn't and adjust accordingly. As long as the end result is your child thinking, imagining, and contributing, we're all good.

Okay, your child is very near school age but isn't quite there yet. Great! That means we have some time, and this is going to be very easy. If your child is already in school, it's going to take a little more work, and you need to act with additional urgency. You also must be prepared for resistance and confusion. If your child is school age, and this hasn't been your normal, it's going to require a little time to adjust and get everyone on board. Be patient, expect some bumps in the road, keep it fun, involve your kid, and keep moving forward.

Assuming you're starting very early, and moving up through the ages, here are some very simple guidelines for how to proceed.

Babies – When your child is a baby, this is extremely simple. Even the stuffiest stuffed-shirt adult can't hold a baby without doing something silly. Do all the typical baby stuff. Peekaboo, playing with hands and feet, rolling, spinning and tossing (safely) are all great for this age. Just be sure to use lots of motion, voice dynamics, and touch. Touch is extremely important for your developing baby. It's important to remember that your child's vision has not fully developed yet, so skip the fine visual details.

Talkers and walkers – Now it's even more fun, and impactful. When your child begins talking there's even more opportunity to interact. Your walking, or crawling, child can play more physically and interactively. Keep it simple. Remember, everything is still new to your child.

Toddlers – Now, there's much more interaction, and your child may even begin to join in. Don't qualify the results for fear of squelching your child's participation. Sure, you can guide a little, but as much as possible, let your child's brain run free.

Early school-age – School material, current events, music, science, and their personal interests begin to dominate now. Your child may even begin to be embarrassed or annoyed by the constant joking and play. Adjust where you need to but still find any possible opportunity to entice your child to think in varied ways, even if it gets a little serious.

Bigger kids – This is when you really need to up your game. Things can get a little challenging. Your kid may tire of your corny jokes. Your success during this time is going to be heavily dependent on how you've done up 'til now. It's also heavily dependent on the relationship you've developed with your child. My kids were accustomed to having me around constantly. I didn't embarrass them, and I kept their trust. That made it easy.

Growing up is all about becoming independent. If there's a little distance between the two of you, that will be more evident than ever now. All of those outside influences, like teachers and peers, may also be working against you. Stay as close to your child as possible, adjust when necessary, and listen intently.

The complexity of life, and your child's endeavors, can be your salvation. Be interested. Study intently what your child is studying, and engage in thought-provoking discussion. This isn't silly thinking. Instead, it's the thinking that you were aiming for all along.

YOU KNOW YOU MADE IT WHEN YOUR KID JOINS IN

Yeah, that's when the real fun begins. The first time your child takes your ideas a step or two farther, and in a direction you didn't consider, it's a banner day. You will see the wheels turning and will know that your child is creating and thinking in brilliant ways. Not to mention that it's just danged fun.

Usually, though, in the beginning, your kid's jokes aren't actually funny. At least not in the classic joke sense. But that doesn't matter. Don't qualify your kid's thoughts. Laugh approvingly and keep your kid on the hook. You're winning when this happens. Don't blow it by being a prude. However, you know your child better than anyone. If it's out of line, you need to offer a little guidance. Just keep it positive.

TWIST EVERYTHING?

Well... not everything but darned close. I never twisted or played with anything that was serious, very important, that could cause a safety issue, or that could hurt someone's feelings. Nearly everything else, including schoolwork, was fair game.

Your kids will pick up on when you're serious and when you're not. That's always a huge teaching moment for social norms and protocol. Of course, kids are notorious for playing and laughing at inappropriate times even when they know better. It's going to happen if you're doing 5 Different Ways or if you're not.

WILL MY KID BECOME A NONSENSE FACTORY?

No. Sure, your kid is going to be silly, often at the worst possible time. That's what kids do. Even if they understand the situation, they often prefer to test the limits rather than abide by social norms. This is why you are there to guide your child and why I said earlier that there must always be an element of logic to 5 Different Ways play.

Simple silliness doesn't fit the bill. Think of it like food. We could easily fill a plate full of silly, inedible junk that would get a laugh but would not nourish your child. Or we could serve a plate that has a sandwich with the filling on the outside, grapes in catsup, veggies carved into menacing creatures, and a drink served in a bowl with a spoon. Everything is twisted so there's plenty to talk and laugh about, but nourishment happens too. There's a measure of logic in everything on the plate, but it's just off from typical enough to encourage some discussion and hopefully some embellishment and imaginative play by your child.

The resultant thinking.

The cover designer for a previous book I wrote encountered a technical problem with the background color. He tried and failed to correct it on many attempts despite his computer and design experience and training. We had a graphics design specialist, who is also a graphic design instructor at a local college, attempt to correct the problem. No luck. He gave up. Then I asked my 16-year-old son to look at it. I did not cloud his thinking by recounting the failed attempts. I only showed him the problem. He paused for a moment (running possibilities through his mind multiple ways) and said, "Why don't you do this?" Poof! Problem solved. And it was incredibly simple. The trained specialists failed by doing what they were trained to do. My son, who is an incredible 5 Different Ways thinker with zero graphic design experience, considered all possibilities and nearly instantly landed on an effective, but way out of the box, solution.

TV, VIDEOS, GAMES, AND TOYS WON'T GET IT DONE

I don't care how interactive the toys and videos are, it's not like interaction with you or some other human (kid or adult). Videos, games, and toys do tend to be outlandish, but they often go too far and too illogical. Interaction with you allows you to guide, correct, and lead (when necessary) your child's thinking. It allows for the subjective effects of seeing your expressions and knowing that you created what's going on. It allows your child to contribute and see your reaction and how you use what your child adds. There is no stinking piece of technology on the planet that will ever measure up to your interaction with your child. And you can screw this up and still get it right. You're being silly after all. Just laugh and start again. There's nothing like modeling how to handle a goof-up in front of your kid.

RESOURCES

Okay, so you don't get it. You're just not a silly person. That's understandable. We're all different. Rigid thinking overtakes us like muscles that lose flexibility. It takes time and effort to get them stretched out and flexible again. Give yourself some time and put in the effort. Let go of the rigid turn-the-kid-into-a-little-adult type thinking and have fun. Making it fun keeps your child engaged and builds powerful, positive subconscious associations with imagination and thinking (and you).

So, you need some help. This is easy. Either hit the web or a bookstore and get some material on puns and so-called "dad jokes." Those are silly, yet intelligent, thinking at its finest. Some of you will scoff and maybe even not find it humorous. That's fine, but your kid will love the stuff. And, in the case of puns, they're not even considered good puns if they're not groan-worthy.

All puns, and most "dad jokes," are the product of thinking past the literal meaning and accepted versions of that which we encounter routinely. And they're the personification of silliness. That's exactly what we want.

Okay, this is a little out there but, against my better judgment, here goes. Stream some Gallagher (the comedian) videos while your kid is out of earshot. This guy is the absolute best at irreverently twisting everything (really, everything) with a strong dose of well-that-makes-sense as well. I still marvel at his frying pan with two handles on opposite sides so it can be easily passed from person to person. I said to keep the kids out of earshot because his language is often not kid-appropriate. You may also find some of his content offensive. And trust me, you don't want your child replicating some of his stunts. You don't want to give away your source either. It's a training film after all.

I'm not telling you to emulate, agree with, or even like Gallagher. I suggest his work only to give you an example of the twisting-with-logic mindset.

THERE WILL BE RESISTANCE

You need to know right now that this is the aspect of brilliance, and brilliance development, that is the most maligned by educators, so-called experts, and anyone who is bent on making your kid "grow up." That includes the sit-up-straight-don't-talk-act-your-age-and-quit-daydreaming factions of the we-have teaching-degrees-and-you-don't-so-we-know-better-than-you crowd.

Did you know that Einstein attributed his brilliant discoveries to play and imagination? Never once did he give any credit to his ability to follow convention, sit up straight, or color within the lines. By the way, did you also know that Einstein was only twenty-six when he published some of his greatest and most influential papers? Yeah, everyone thinks it was that wirehaired old guy. Brilliance is not reserved for our later years. And he first started on the path to those great discoveries through vivid imagination play at the age of 16 when he explored speed as it relates to a beam of light. That's right. Daydreaming and play are where all that great thinking began. They're also what he used throughout his career. Too bad he didn't have someone there to tell him to stop that nonsense (insert eye-roll). This is why I said earlier that we're not going to stop, especially because someone who doesn't understand brilliance tells us to stop.

"The desire to arrive finally at logically connected concepts is the emotional basis of a vague play with basic ideas. This combinatory or associative play seems to be the essential feature in productive thought."

-Albert Einstein

They don't even try to get it.

It always struck me as interesting that through all of the years that my two kids were in school (I started homeschooling at 6th and 8th grades), not one teacher ever asked me or my kids about how they managed to perform so much better than the rest of the class. They were consistently at the top of their class (first-in-class recognition started in 1st grade), they won many academic and artistic competitions, they blew away their EOGs, and they made it all look easy. But they did things differently, so I was often called in by teachers who tried to tell me that I was messing up my kids. Each time the teacher would enumerate the ways my kids didn't follow convention. I would respond by recounting how much better they performed than typical. The teacher would always agree but then would immediately go back to complaining about my kids not following convention. I became very adept at aggressively ignoring their complaints.

By the way. I often offered to clue the teachers in on how I did it but never once did a teacher ever want to even hear about it. "No! Different! Run away!"

WHY THIS ISN'T LIKE THE OLD PAPER CLIP TEST

You might be thinking that 5 Different Ways is similar to the old paper clip test where you think of as many ways as you can to use a paperclip. The paper clip test is commonly used to help people connect with, and develop their creative powers. A 5 Different Ways way of thinking would certainly help you perform well on the paper clip test but the two are very different.

The paper clip test, and tests like it, are very narrow in scope. They're okay for assessing your ability to think beyond the norm but they fail miserably when used as a way to develop thinking for creativity and problem-solving. This approach treats thinking like a toolbox filled with thinking tools. When you need to think "outside the box," you reach in for a tool and put it to work. Sometimes you've used the tool recently, so you do fairly well with it. Other times, the tool is rusted and unfamiliar. You spend as much time cleaning it up and trying to remember how to use it as you do actually putting it to work.

This contrived, planned, and lesson-type thinking is only moderately effective. 5 Different Ways results in a whole-brain, whole-knowledge, natural way of thinking that happens nearly effortlessly with no need to be switched on and off.

HOW WILL MY KID EVER SORT THIS OUT?

Have you ever thought about what your kid already sorts out every day? How does any kid ever figure out what's baby talk and what's real language? And with all of the "I'm gonna get you," faux threats to the inappropriate things they do that we laugh at, encourage, and call cute, how does any kid ever sort out what is and isn't socially acceptable behavior? Then watch a little bit of kid's TV or streamed programming and see if any of it resembles anything normal. Yet, most kids sort it all out with ease.

You don't need to worry when you're doing 5 Different Ways. Your child will easily pick up on your inflection and delivery. It's a huge part of learning to communicate and function socially.

Your child will learn when it's time to be serious, what matters, and what doesn't. That doesn't mean that your kid won't laugh right in the face of all that, but that's what kids do.

ARE THERE RISKS OR DOWNSIDES TO THIS?

Yup. The biggest is becoming an overthinker. Overthinking leads to everything from inaction to missed opportunities to the scrapping of ideas that were perfectly fine. Your child may need some guidance to understand that perfection is not always possible, and that progress is essential.

The next potential problems is intolerance of errors and apathy. Your kid is going to see so much that others miss, and there's a good chance your kid won't keep quiet about it. More guidance will be necessary as you teach your child this and other ways to manage social situations.

If I hear just one more person say that something is better "then" something else... Just one more...

THIS MAY NOT SIT WELL WITH SOME OF YOU

You need to like being corrected by your child. Many parents consider being corrected by a kid to be an afront to their authority. Sure, you've got to teach your kid tact, but don't shoot your kid down every time your kid knows something that you don't. Flush your ego down the toilet and be proud that your kid is on the ball. Take the opportunity to learn something. Most of all, don't make your child feel like being smart is a negative.

WHY IS THERE NO LIST OF EXAMPLES?

I have sprinkled in a few small examples, but this isn't about you copying me. 5 Different Ways must be relevant to you and your child and your relationship. You have a personality and your child is developing one. Relax and let it happen. You've got this.

THE BOTTOM LINE

Constantly keep your kid on his or her intellectual toes. Make everything a thinking situation. To keep your child involved and engaged, make it fun and silly. To keep it relevant and effective, always base your silliness on an element of logic. Push the limits and ideas as far as you like. Let your child join in. Don't overthink it. Just play and have fun. Play is when learning happens, the mind expands, relationships are strengthened, memories are formed, and brilliance is built. Do not pass this off as just play. This is how your child will develop the most important thinking habit he or she will ever have or need.

7

FOCUS AND ATTENTION SPAN

Not like you think.

THIS IS NOT ABOUT YOUR CHILD ACQUIRING some newfound, miraculous superhuman power of laser-guided focus and unlimited attention span. This is about not training your child to not focus and to have a very short attention span. Very often, the problem is not that your child has the inability to focus. It's more likely that your child is conditioned to have a very short attention span. That's great news because that means that focus and the ability to pay attention are teachable. It really can be that simple. Your child's brilliant mind has got this.

SOMETIMES IT'S NOT THAT SIMPLE

Attention disorders can be very complex and are often associated with other serious conditions and disorders. There is growing belief among psychology professionals that attention disorders are over-diagnosed. Regardless, if you suspect your child is suffering from a medical or psychological condition consult, with medical and psychology professionals immediately.

HOW LONG YOUR CHILD'S ATTENTION SPAN SHOULD BE...

The experts agree about as much as in-laws talking politics at a Thanksgiving dinner. Most commonly, they say one minute per year in age, but that's extremely ambiguous and leaves out a lot of important factors like distractions, interest, expectations, etc. Other experts dismiss the one minute per year in age and say that attention span is dependent on the task at hand which does take into consideration distractions, interest, expectations, etc.

Your child should have the ability to apply his or herself to a mental-age-appropriate task long enough to complete it. Huh? Okay, that's a little ambiguous too. The problem is that every child is different, and every task is different. Individuals have different mental ages, and they have different interests.

The real goal is to acquire the ability to discipline one's self to focus on a task, subject, or event, even if it is not desired or of interest. Eventually, that would be for as long as is required to accomplish relevant goals. That's what it takes to get things done and getting things done is what brilliant people do.

ARE ATTENTION SPANS GETTING SHORTER?

Who knows? Scientists who study such things don't know. And don't trust those Internet articles that throw numbers around authoritative-like. Do a little research, and you will find that they're suspect at best. There's no consensus at all, so the heck with it. Let's go with this instead. Maybe attention spans are getting shorter and maybe they're not. But attention spans are definitely shorter than they can be. How do I know that?

Because almost no one trains their attention span, and humans can always improve when they apply themselves. That, I hope, we can agree on.

DON'T BELIEVE ATTENTION SPANS ARE SHORT?

Give yourself a little test. This is extremely simple. Just close your eyes and concentrate on the darkness you see in front of you. Think of absolutely nothing but that darkness without letting a single other thought in. How long did you last? If you're like most people, an intrusive thought happened before you even got settled in. That's usually in the two to five-second range. Sure, concentrating would be easier if you were engaged in a physical task, but sometimes, we just need to think. This quick test shows that it's not exactly easy. Keep this in mind when you're trying to get your kid, whose brain isn't fully developed and who couldn't care less about learning the ABCs, to concentrate.

By the way, if you practice, you can become much better at shutting down those intrusive thoughts. This comes in handy when you want to get some shut-eye.

I BELIEVE WE ARE EARNING OUR SHORT ATTENTION SPANS

It seems the only time people have unlimited focus is when they're looking at their phones while driving. There are two major players involved in attention span. Interest (includes perceived value) and conditioning. If your child is interested in something, the kitchen can explode into flames, and your child won't even look up. If there is no interest or perceived value to your child, poor conditioning can take over and make it a struggle for your child to focus no matter how much effort is involved.

When we're not driven by purpose, we do what we are

conditioned to do. The results are never as good if we let that happen by default. A huge part of being brilliant is the deliberate development of intelligent behavior. Us adults can decide to take ourselves on as a project due to perceived benefit. Children, on the other hand, are going to do what brings them pleasure. It's up to you to guide them, trick them, and otherwise condition them to improve.

The really good news is that the exploding kitchen situation shows us that your child is indeed capable of excellent focus and attention. So, why doesn't your child exhibit that capability when asked to practice multiplication tables? Really, you have to ask?

MTV*

I first became aware of the conditioning-by-default problem watching the MTV* (Music Television) cable channel way back in the 80s. Yeah, I'm old, so what? Have you ever watched one of those videos? Images remain on the screen for fractions of a second. Sometimes very small fractions of a second. It's like a multisensory stimulation strobe light. Those videos are perfect training for attention span destruction. They're entertaining, intriguing, often irreverent, they're multisensory, and most importantly, they evoke strong emotion. *"More sensory input! I need more sensory input!"* The kids loved it, and many parents were happy to park their kids in front of it for hours.

Fast-forward to now. Music videos retain some of their appeal and they haven't changed a bit except that they've become shorter. I wonder why? But music videos have been eclipsed by the attention-span killing mega monsters. Video streaming

*MTV is a registered trademark of Viacom International, Inc.

services, video games, and instant information via the Internet make music videos look like a minor blip on the radar.

Video games – You might argue that the fact that teenagers, and even younger children, will play for thirty-six hours straight without a bathroom break is indicative of an exceptional attention span. I can see how you might draw that conclusion. That's not the case though. What's actually happening is that your child is drawn to a constant stream of multisensory stimulus and an almost addictive need for satisfaction by reaching ever deeper levels of the game. That's not superior attention span, that's addictive behavior.

Streaming video – Gone are the days of waiting for Saturday morning cartoons. Now you can get your mindless content instantly 24/7. Yay!

Smartphones – Now we don't even have to wait to get home to get our video games and streaming video fixes. Oh, and we don't have to wait to make a phone call either. Yeah, smartphones still make calls too.

Some surveys indicate that the average American spends five hours a day on their mobile devices. That's probably very conservative. Kids, that includes very young ones and teens, nearly live online now. Sadly, many of them are literally becoming addicted to their technology to the point of being socially and mentally debilitating.

A SHORT ATTENTION SPAN MIGHT NOT BE A BAD THING

Does your kid seem to not stay with anything for very long? Maybe your child is just extremely intelligent. Very intelligent people get bored quickly, and they avoid simple boring things like other people avoid root canals. A very young bored child won't know to tell you that something is boring. Instead, the child will rebel or simply find something more interesting to do. It's amazing how often that other "more interesting" thing is annoying, destructive, or otherwise maddening to the adult in the room. That leads to frustration for all involved and some pretty negative associations in your kid's head.

It's very important for you to understand that your child isn't misbehaving on purpose (okay, somethings but not always). The kid is just seeking stimuli that satisfies the curiosity and inquisitiveness of high intelligence. And your kid can't tolerate a slow pace that doesn't match his or her thinking speed. This is exactly why I spent my elementary and middle school years hearing a constant drone of, "PAY ATTENTION!" and "STOP TALKING!" from every single teacher I ever reluctantly sat in front of.

If this is the case with your child, you need to help your child channel that intelligence, and you need to help your child learn to tolerate the mundane (good luck with this one). Channeling requires guidance more than instruction. All that pent-up intelligence needs to be expended in a multisensory chain of learning, failing, and exploring. Provide lots of stimulating tasks that lead to productive learning in order to direct those intellectual energies. Increase the complexity as you see boredom creeping in. Again, guide but instruct as little as possible. Let your kid expend as much thinking power as possible.

Let your child work quickly and bounce from experience to experience but also gently encourage staying on task just a little longer at times. This is to help your child begin to understand the benefits of focus and tolerance of what is perceived to be boring. It helps if there is a payoff in the form of an accomplishment or some new interesting bit of learning to further satisfy that inquisitive mind.

Be careful to not fall into the very intelligent child's trap. Kids can read us adults way better than we often think. I remember my mother talking to a five-year-old at my niece's birthday party. The girl's mother had told her an hour earlier that they had to leave. When asked by my mother how she got to stay, the young lady replied, "I pulled the whining and crying routine on her (mom). It works every time." Just remember this, when your child throws mud on the wall it isn't necessarily art no matter how much your young Jackson Pollock says it is.

OVERLOAD

If you want to knock focus out cold just overload your child (that includes fun and not so fun activities). Then chastise your child for failing to focus to ensure that the kid understands the meaning of hopelessness. We tend to overload our kid's day with dozens of activities we nearly kill ourselves trying to cram in. We call it making the most of life. I think we're missing life when we overdo it. You're definitely not doing your kid's attention span any favors.

By the way. It's not necessary for your school-age kid to study ten hours a day without looking up (that goes for your toddler too). I homeschooled my two kids from grades six and eight. We typically spent no more than 2½ hours a day on formal school. No homework too. I did sneak in a lot of learning throughout the rest of the day by just including them and telling them about whatever I wished.

SLEEP

No one can focus when they're sleep-deprived. Kids are worse than adults. Very young children don't even recognize that they're too sleepy to function. Teenagers aren't much better. Chronic sleep deprivation is even worse. It often manifests as apathy, belligerence, anger, poor school performance, etc. That often results in punishment which just exacerbates the situation. Obviously, your child needs to get enough sleep. That's not always easy, but it needs to happen if your child is going to make the most of his or her brain. Focus and attention span are absolutely dependent on proper sleep.

And... wait for it... your child needs to... WAKE UP WITHOUT AN ALARM CLOCK (that includes anything a parent does to wake the kid). We humans sleep in cycles of around 90 minutes. Wake us up in the middle of a cycle, and our brain performance and focus are toast. Do this constantly, and your child will have little hope of being brilliant. Your child, and you, need to get to bed at a time that will permit you to wake up naturally. Really, I'm not going all new-age-hippy on you. This is science. Your body needs to come out of a sleep cycle naturally when the required amount of sleep has been completed. That can be a little different for everyone and every kid.

Your kid getting enough sleep is a piece of cake when they're very young because you welcome the break, and most very young kids sleep a lot anyway (unless it's nighttime of course). Then school comes. No matter how late they got to bed because of the epic battle your kid waged, it's up and at 'em at 5:30 am.

Let's go over that again. Our sleep cycles are approximately 90 minutes. Waking up, especially in an alarming way, before a cycle completes will leave anyone unable to function at their full mental capacity. It will leave a kid cranky, belligerent, and intellectually impaired. Kids require a lot of sleep, and they need it on a consistent schedule. Get them to bed early enough to wake on their own and make that bedtime consistent. Yes, I know that I've asked the impossible. But, if you can make it happen, the payoff is huge. You homeschoolers have a very distinct advantage here with no school bus to catch. Make the most of it and let your kid sleep in.

SO, HOW DO WE FIX SHORT ATTENTION SPANS?

It's never going to be easy or natural to get your kid to happily pay attention to mundane, boring, unfun stuff. That's why you need to work on conditioning very early. The idea here is to make it as natural as possible to focus, so it doesn't seem like some undeserved punishment is being thrust upon them when you require them to pay attention. And because we're always better at that which is within our "normal."

Concentrating on undesirable tasks is always going to require effort, but if we make the default range (the normal) as high as possible, less extra effort will be required for demanding tasks. It just becomes what your child does. In many countries, kids eat fish for breakfast. That's weird to many of us but perfectly normal for them. It all has to do with the normal that you create. By starting early enough and staying consistent, you can create nearly any normal that you wish.

In short, we're trying to make your child's normal attention span long enough so that when a demanding task comes along, they just need to ramp it up a couple of notches rather than having to bring it up from the subbasement.

WAYS TO MAKE IT HAPPEN

This is not a step-by-step, how-to process. This is a long-term project that will happen in small and large ways throughout your child's daily life. Remember, you are establishing a "normal," not interrupting the day for lessons.

Deal with failure. It seems like the more you want your kid to focus, the less that will happen. It's in their DNA. Sure, sometimes it's defiance and misbehavior. Often though, it's disinterest, ignorance of value, and an immature brain. Be as patient as possible.

Know that it's trainable. Just knowing that focus and attention span are trainable gives you the ability to start from a positive position. It may not happen quickly, and you may not reach the goal you set for your child. If you miss your goal but your child reaches their full potential, that's a win.

Expectations – Keep your expectations, age and mental-age, appropriate and reasonable. Remember that you're not dealing with a little adult. Your child has no concept of the importance of any of this. That will be learned much later. Then there's the fact that your child's brain is far from fully developed.

Stay on a task - Pick times to stay on one subject, game, or task. Don't hide in a quiet room. Instead, just let life happen around you and your child without leaving the game or task. Demonstrate the ability to persevere while taking your child along for the ride. This is one that you can do with even very young children.

Make eye contact – "Look at me!" "Watch!" Kids want your attention for everything. Most of what they have on their mind is trivial, meaningless, and worthless... to us adults. We carry right on with what we're doing and let our kids beg for our attention. STOP IT! Right now! Really, I mean right now. Drop what you're doing. Turn and look your child in the eye and give your undivided attention. Show your kid what it means to pay attention. At the same time, you're telling your kid that they're of value to you. How great is that?

Right now, you're thinking that this is a great way to turn your kid into a spoiled, narcissistic nightmare. I didn't say to put your kid on a pedestal and drop to your knees. I said to just treat your child like you would treat anyone else. And you don't have to do it every time they come to you. Of course, your child needs to learn manners and that there's an appropriate time for things. You can still do that and give your kid your undivided attention often enough to model what it's like to pay attention to someone when that person is of value to you.

Make it payoff - Assign tasks with rewards for efficient completion. Start small with things like reading a book, drawing a picture, or building something with blocks. The reward can be anything small that motivates your kid. Why small? Big rewards are for big accomplishments. Leave room to go up.

Bored games - No, that is not a typo. It's okay if your child gets a little bored while playing board games. Board games that require thinking, strategy, and memory are great for slowing things down and practicing focus and attention. Just learning to wait when Cousin Zeke requires fifteen minutes to take his turn is a lesson in patience and perseverance. Help your child understand that downtime in the game is when you observe and strategize. The classic games are the best for this purpose. Hippos eating marbles, dropping discs in slots, and boxing robots are not going to cut it.

Tedious projects – This one is a little paradoxical. The idea is to encourage your child to take on a project that requires substantial time (relative to what your kid is accustomed to) to teach the rewards of focus. Painting, sculpture, model building, building with blocks, and the like fit the bill well. The paradoxical part is that if your kid happily takes on the project that means that it was attractive already. That means your child didn't so much learn tolerance as display a desire. Still, it's a win if your child exercises focus and the ability to complete the task.

Distractions, distractions – Resist the temptation to always silence the room when you're working on focus and attention. Sure, your kid needs to learn that there are times when you need to get away from the world to get things done. The ability to tune out distractions is important too and much more applicable to daily life. Brilliant people are great at getting things done while the world swirls around them. Homeschoolers are very familiar with this. My kids did their work at the kitchen table while the dogs barked, the doorbell rang, and I took the occasional business call. They learned to deal with it in real-time and, as young adults, they're incredible at working through distractions.

Take breaks – No one can do something fanatically forever even if it is enjoyable. Your brain needs a break. Understanding the value of a reasonable break (as opposed to an excuse to quit) is just as valuable as focus and attention.

Teach the value – This is a tough one for kids of all ages. If you can pull it off though it's gold. If you can help your child understand the value of focus and maintaining attention to complete a less-than-fun task, your child will be much more likely to persevere. Obviously, this is for older children who can conceptualize. Making this happen is going to be very dependent on your child's personality too. This requires leading, as opposed to lecturing, and modeling rather than requiring.

Give 'em a shoutout – When you see your older child focusing and demonstrating a longer attention span point it out. Not in a condescending, "See! You told me you couldn't do it" way. Point it out in a way-to-go you've-got-this tone. Every kid likes recognition.

MULTITASKING

Ahh, the myth of multitasking. Have you ever seen one of those people who can keep a bunch of plates spinning on the tops of sticks? They run back and forth refreshing the spin of the ones that are slowing in an ever-increasingly futile effort to keep them all going. While one plate gets attention, the others are all beginning to fall. That's your brain on "multitasking." The plate spinner usually quits before everything crashes down. Multitaskers often don't.

The problem is that our brains can do only one thing at a time. When we think we're paying attention to more than one thing, we're actually switching rapidly between them. In general, this is frowned upon when it comes to efficient and effective use of your intellectual resources. However, being able to manage multiple tasks and data inputs rapidly can come in very handy for people like fighter pilots, stockbrokers, emergency management personnel, and parents of triplets.

So, learning to switch between multiple tasks quickly and

unexpectedly while retaining the status and needs of the abandoned tasks is a great skill to develop. This is a skill that brilliant people will put to work when necessary, not as a way of routinely overloading themselves.

There are lots of ways you can help your child develop the ability to intelligently manage multiple tasks. As always, the goal is for it to be natural, so no lessons. Just do it. As for when to start, that is going to be very individual. This is not something that you want to start with a very young child. It could just lead to frustration and confusion. I believe the child should be intellectually mature enough to understand the goal if you were to explain it. I'm not telling you to explain the goal because that would turn this into a lesson, and that's something we don't want.

Pardon the interruption - Interrupt something your child is enjoying and will want to complete with something equally or more enjoyable. Stay on the second activity long enough to tax your child's memory of the first just a bit and then switch back. Rinse and repeat.

Two games – Play two games at once. It can be simple like playing tic-tac-toe or checkers, against two players. Have your child alternate turns between the two opponents. As your child acclimates, you can increase the playing pace. You may even want to bump it up to three or four opponents as your child advances.

"I've got so many things going at once, they're all at a standstill."
-Anonymous

Most importantly, as your child matures and enters school, ensure that your child understands the difference in being able to manage multiple tasks and multitasking. It's also extremely important to help your child understand how to prioritize tasks, how to say no, and how to delegate in order to avoid the need or desire to multitask.

THE BOTTOM LINE

There are two types of attention and focus that we're working on. Single-minded attention to complete an undesired task in spite of wanting to do something else and the ability to rapidly switch our focus when demands require it.

Keep it all a part of your normal life. Sit-down-and-stare-at-me lessons are a waste of time. Remember that every kid is different and that your child does not understand the value of focus and attention span or the value of the task. That all must be learned. And most importantly, remember that your child is not a little adult and that your child's brain is far from fully developed. Take the small wins, deal with the losses, and keep moving forward.

8

GIVE YOUR KID CONTROL

Yeah, you read that right.

OKAY... NOW THIS GUY HAS LOST HIS MIND. No, really! You've got to hear me out! When do you work better? When your boss says, "You've got this" and leaves you to it or when your micromanaging boss breathes down your neck and questions your every move? When are you happiest, most confident, most content, and most motivated? Right, when you feel that you are in control. Your kid is no different.

Brilliant people tend to know what they're doing; they work well independently, and they despise being questioned by someone who doesn't know as much as they do. Or anyone else for that matter. A huge part of this is the feeling of being in control. Notice I said "feeling" of being in control. Interestingly, we don't need to actually exert control to enhance our performance. This is a somewhat strange, but very powerful, way to improve your relationship with your child while building brilliance as well.

DO YOU REALLY MEAN I SHOULD GIVE MY KID CONTROL?

Well... Yes and no. We are talking about a kid here, and your child's safety is more important than anything. And it's very important to maintain your authority as parent or guardian. But there are major benefits available by giving your child a sense of control. As your child gets older, that will transition to actual control with your supervision. For now, though, it's only a sense of being in control.

BUT WHY?

As older kids and adults, brilliant people tend to be independent thinkers. They're typically self-motivated and self-driven to perform well. They're also human. Because they typically know that they know what they're doing, and they very often have their own way of doing things. They have great disdain for being micromanaged. Brilliant people want to be in control (actually, everyone does). Want to get the most out of a brilliant person (or anyone for that matter)? Just give them a sense of being in control and get out of the way. Want to flush every bit of that down the toilet? Question and micromanage them.

When you're helping your young child develop and maintain their brilliance, you need your child on your side. You need your child to be motivated and working toward independence in thought and mindset. That requires a good working relationship between the two of you, and that's not going to happen if your child is not happy, confident, and self-motivated.

Giving your child control does it all. It accomplishes what we need during these early years as they're developing their brilliance, and it solidifies the mindsets and habits that will support their brilliance as older kids and through adulthood.

HOW DOES THIS WORK?

There's a lot of science to back this up. As you know by now, I'm not big on scientific studies, but this concept is so counter to conventional parental thinking that I need someone to have my back. So, before we get into how this is going to work, let's look at some of the science.

THE SCIENCE

In the late 60s and early 70s, several studies were conducted by David Glass and Jerome E. Singer that explored how humans perform in relation to their perception of being in control. The results were consistent and exactly what most of us would intuitively expect (for us adults anyway), and I believe they have direct relevance to your child's intellectual development and pursuit of brilliance.

The experiments were very simple. Test subjects (adults in their early 20s) were asked to perform simple tasks, such as very basic math, proofreading, and attempting to solve insoluble puzzles while being exposed to loud very distracting noise. The noise was a combination of people speaking Spanish and Armenian along with the sounds of a mechanical typewriter, mechanical calculator, and a mimeograph machine (a prehistoric copy machine) (Glass et al., "Psychic Cost" 201). The resulting noise was a seriously distracting unintelligible roar.

In addition to their interest in the effects of a sense of control, the researchers also explored the effects of predictability on performance. I will discuss the very important implications of predictability later in this chapter.

Over the course of several studies, subjects were tested under varying conditions. In groups, they were tested with no noise (as a control group), with randomly (unpredictable) occurring noise, with noise at fixed (predictable) intervals, with varying noise volume levels, and with the ability to turn the noise off.

As you would expect, across the board, those who were subjected to the distracting noise performed poorly when compared to the groups that were tested with no distracting noise. Duh, right? Also, as would be expected, most subjects adapted to the distraction over time and improved their performance but never to the level of the non-noise group.

For this discussion, though, the most important group is the group that was given control over their situation. This group was provided a button with which they could turn off the distracting noise. They weren't just given control in passing, though. The researchers gave the test subjects very specific, and interesting, instructions for the use of the button.

The test subjects were heavily influenced against turning off the noise but with emphasis that it was okay to do so. They were told that "they could at any time terminate the noise for the remainder of the session" and that "the experimenter preferred that they did not press the switch, but the choice was entirely up to them." The study authors stated, "The latter half of the instruction was given particular emphasis in order to induce forces against pressing the switch while at the same time giving the subjects a feeling that they could press it, if they so desired" (Glass et al., "Psychic Cost" 206).

Not surprisingly, the group who had control, in the form of the button to turn off the noise, performed much better on all tasks. They made nearly five times as many attempts to solve the insoluble puzzles and they made much fewer proofreading errors (Glass et al., "Psychic Cost" 207). So, those subjects who were given control over their situation performed much better than those who did not. That's even though they were told that it was preferred that they not exert that control.

Now, here's the payoff. Drumroll, please...! Not one single solitary test subject pressed the button! Not one. Did you get that? Not one. No one turned off the noise (Glass et al., "Psychic Cost" 206). Just the feeling of control was enough to elevate their performance well above the other (non-button) group.

But wait, there's more!

A second study added another level of complexity. I believe this one has direct implications for you as a parent. In this study, the test subjects were given indirect control over the noise (the exact same noise as in the previous study). The test subjects had the ability to signal a second person to ask them to turn the noise off. The tasks they were given were identical to those in the previous study (Glass et al., "Behavioral Consequences" 248). The purpose of this study was to evaluate the effect of having access to someone who has control over the noise (Glass et al., "Behavioral Consequences" 245).

The instructions were very similar as well, stressing that it was okay to stop the noise. These test subjects were even deceived into believing that others had indeed exerted that control and had pressed the button relieving them of the annoying noise. "Some people who come here do in fact activate the light" referring to the signal to stop the noise. The researchers also added, "Whether you press the button is up to you" and "We'd prefer that you do not, but the decision is up to you." They gave special emphasis to that last part of the instructions (Glass et al., "Behavioral Consequences" 247).

Just like before, those who were subjected to the noise performed very poorly when compared to those who did not have to suffer through it. And those who had control over the noise, although indirect, performed much better. "The present experiment shows that the perception of indirect control (through access to another who presumably has direct control) also meliorates the postadaptive effects. The important percept seems to be knowledge that one can contact the person in power even if there is no guarantee that he will come to one's assistance. Having access to "the top" appears to be a sufficient condition for inducing feelings of control and easing the costs of adaptation" (Glass et al., "Behavioral Consequences" 253).

Drum roll again, please...! And once again, not one single solitary subject requested that the noise be turned off. Not one (Glass et al., "Behavioral Consequences" 254).

WHAT DOES THIS MEAN TO US?

Giving a human being (your kid is one of those) a sense of control (perceived control) is enough to enhance performance even in the presence of circumstances that would otherwise impair performance. There were many theories posited in the discussion sections of those studies that attempted to explain why a sense of control contributed to better performance, but I'm only interested in your child.

While none of the test subjects were children, I believe the results are still relevant to kids as much as anyone else. I know it's been true in my experience. When it comes to children, I believe the effect is primarily the result of two factors, the feeling of control itself and the fact that someone has expressed confidence in them. In the studies discussed above, the researchers were very careful to ensure that they were leaving the decision entirely of the hands of the test subject. Kids feed on attention and, to a child, expressing confidence in them is nuclear-powered attention. I bet you can remember right now a time in your childhood when someone expressed confidence in you, and I'd bet a little more that it lit quite a fire in your belly.

Taking advantage of this effect will move your child toward brilliance (as an independent thinker and doer). It will also improve your relationship with your child as your child experiences a sense of control as well as your confidence. It can also give your kid some of the positive memories like you have of someone expressing confidence in you. Of course, considering that we're working with a child here, it can also go all kinds of sideways at times. But that's just life when raising a child. You and your child will learn from mistakes and missteps. Move forward and play until you win.

I believe the effects of indirect control are very important to you as a parent or guardian because you are the go-to person in your child's life. You are the person at "the top" that your child depends on. You are the person who provides the perception of control as well. To maintain your relationship with your child you must maintain your child's confidence in you as that person who will come through for them when needed. That trust is vitally important. This all serves to instill in your child the confidence to perform even in adverse conditions. Having your confidence and knowing that you will come through for them if needed serves to solidify your relationship with your child as well as supporting brilliant performance.

MAKING IT HAPPEN

This can start very early. It's easy. Any time your child has a responsibility to do something is an opportunity to give your kid a sense of control. Give your instructions, express confidence, then get out of the way. Praise success and guide when there's failure. Expressing confidence cannot be overstated. You must ensure that your child understands that the choice is his or hers to make and that you trust that choice.

The early years - In the very early years, it is truly only a sense of control that you're giving. That's for safety because there's a high probability of failure. You're always going to be watching. Stealthily watching, but still watching. Additionally, in the very early years, it's important to set your child up to win. Confidence is much easier to destroy than it is to build. Don't make it too easy though. Your child needs to experience a sense of accomplishment that only come with a perceived challenge.

All you need to do is tell your child what is expected and then express your confidence that the kid has got this. Just pick a simple task like putting toys away, selecting the lunch menu, making the rules for a game, selecting what to play, and the like. Then step back and watch.

If, and when, it goes wrong, deal with it gently. Any hint of a you-blew-it attitude will be like a neon sign to your kid. When it goes right, give a smile and a, "See, I knew you could do it," and an, "I'm proud of you." Be careful with praise. If you make everything a big deal, then nothing is a big deal. Make sure you keep a little in reserve for big accomplishments. It also doesn't hurt to tell others about your kid's accomplishment while your kid is present. What kid doesn't love that?

As they get a little older – The scenario stays the same as in the early years. The tasks just become more complicated. Additionally, more tasks move into the expected behavior category. Those that are praiseworthy are fewer and more complex. That part about not having a you-blew-it attitude is even more important now. You can praise your child a hundred times with modest effect. Give 'em one you-blew-it and you've created an indelible memory that eclipses hundreds of compliments.

Early school years – The tasks are increasing in number and complexity. School assignments and more complex social situations have entered the mix. It's easier now to select what to praise because the expected performance list covers most tasks. Most giving-control events are going to be school, chore, and social interaction oriented.

The best part of this age is that you can have some deep and meaningful interaction with your kid when giving instructions as well as when assessing performance. Give your kid some respect. No pedestals are necessary, and you need to maintain the chain of command, but a little common respect and eye contact can fit in easily. Your reactions are more important than ever. Keep it positive but truthful. Maintaining trust and belief is extremely important. Your praise will not be valued if it is not believed. Your admonishment will often be exaggerated in your kid's head. And your body language always speaks louder than your words.

Safety First
What could possibly go wrong with giving control? Well, just about anything. Just because you're giving your child a feeling of being in control, does not mean you should let your guard down. Always keep your child and everyone else safe.

THE BIG SECRET (A LITTLE REPETITION)

Especially with young children, you don't need to actually give control. All that's needed is a sense of control. Remember, no one in the studies ever actually exerted control. As I've eluded to several times in this chapter, you can always watch or otherwise monitor. But! And this is a big but. Be extremely careful. Kids can pick up on deception like a dog smelling that bacon you're hiding in your pocket. If your kid catches you not actually trusting them, this all falls like a house of cards in a tornado. You might get away with it a couple of times with a very young child but don't count on it. Be very, very careful.

A LITTLE MORE ABOUT HOW IT CAN GO WRONG

Kids are going to fail and they're going to let you down, sometimes fairly often and in big ways. So, it's a good idea to start small and work your way up. Sometimes your kid will outright take advantage of you (planning and scheming can be a sign of intelligence, by the way). They're kids. What did you expect? Don't blow it by freaking out. You expected it, right? It also doesn't mean that you can't try again. And again. No kid is going to tire of having their parent express confidence and belief in them.

Often, though, your child will come through for you. In the beginning, pile on the praise. As time goes on, back it down to just-what-I-expected level. Don't shrug it off though. Just an affirming head nod with a faint grin, or a, "thanks" will do it. That implies more confidence. Your child will take the bait and will cherish the respect, even if your kid doesn't say so.

Of course, sometimes things go so bad that you're forced to dole out a little punishment. Just be sure to keep it reasonable, or you will lose any gain you may have made. And be sure to read the section below about being predictable. Being predictable is all-important when things go wrong.

Warning!
Never use anything educational or learning oriented as punishment. Never create a negative association with learning.

THE DOUBLE-EDGED SWORD

This giving a sense of control stuff dovetails with high expectations. Having high expectations is a great way to express confidence in your kid. That leads to higher-level performance tasks, and that inevitably leads to pressure on the kid. That's because we tend to hold smarter, higher-performing kids to higher standards. Now the kid gets in trouble for not succeeding when the failure was above other kids' achievements. That can easily lead to the, "I wish I wasn't smart" reaction. That proceeds straight to the darned-if-I-do, darned-if-I-don't feeling.

Despite my best efforts to avoid it, I ended up there with both of my kids more than once. We got past it in short order, but I was left wondering just how long it was in my kids' heads before they ever said anything. My guess is it was there quite a while. This raising kids to be brilliant stuff is a tightrope walk. You're never going to get it perfect. I suspect it was my body language that betrayed me. That's all it takes.

There's another way it can go wrong. In your head, you're blissfully giving your child control and proudly watching your offspring rise to the challenge. In your child's head, it can be more like, "Everything gets dumped on me, and why am I being abandoned again?" Yeah, it can be a tight-rope walk.

Step back every now and then and assess where you are and what you're expecting of your child. Sometimes you need to back off and let the kid be a kid. Sometimes you back off for a little while and then hit it again. Other times you need to throw your pursuit in a dumpster and let your kid off the hook.

Stay objective and communicate with your child as much as possible. I know, they usually won't tell you what they're thinking. Read your kid as best you can. When you mess up, it's a great time to own up to it and let your kid know you're human. That's also a great time to teach them how to handle failure.

BE PREDICTABLE

Earlier, I mentioned the implications of being predictable. I have no desire to tell you how to parent your child, but when there are basic factors that will impact your child's brilliance, I must discuss them.

In the studies that I referenced above, the researchers also explored the effects of predictability of the disturbing distractions in relation to performance and the subjects' ability to adapt to that distraction. To accomplish this, they tested one group with noise occurring at random times and another group with noise at predictable intervals (Glass et al., "Psychic Cost" 201).

They found that random noise resulted in much poorer performance. Subjects receiving the same annoying noise at predictable intervals were better able to adapt to the audio assault (Glass et al., "Psychic Cost" 208). Similar results have been observed with animals that were subjected to mild shocks at random vs. predictable intervals.

The point is that even when the situation is bad, we can often manage it if it is at least predictable. If we don't know when it's coming or why, everything goes to that hot place in a handbasket. As parents, we often react to things that are in our heads even though our kids are oblivious. This goes for even older kids and young adults. They just have different agendas and priorities than we do. This gives the kid that random assault feeling. You must be predictable. By that, I mean that your actions and reactions must be consistent, equal to the situation, and understandable by your kid.

For anything in this book to be successful, you need a good relationship with your child. That's for your sanity and your child's intellectual development. Of course, there will always be bumps in the road. Those bumps sometimes warrant punishment in some form whether it is a simple talk, beratement, or something more serious. When you must punish your child, be predictable and consistent.

You can always surprise your child with warranted and earned praise with zero adverse effects!

THE BOTTOM LINE

When it's appropriate, give your child a sense of control. Progress until you are actually giving control. Of course, stealthily watch and keep everything safe. Do all of this in an air of expressing confidence in your child. Reasonably praise success, guide and teach through failures, and deal with egregious behavior reasonably and predictably.

9

DELAYING GRATIFICATION

Is it really all it's cracked up to be?

BEING IMPULSIVE RARELY ENDS WELL. MAYBE you get lucky occasionally, but for the most part, it's a very risky way to live life. It's certainly not brilliant behavior because, by definition, very little thought is involved. Although it can happen very quickly, being brilliant requires a measure of self-control, introspection, and deliberate analysis.

Children rarely exhibit exceptional self-control. There is much debate about how much this is genetic and how much is learned. Luckily there have been a bunch of studies that confuse the heck out of this for us. Really, there's been a lot of testing and analysis, but the opinions are all over the map, although they do mostly agree that self-control is a good thing. Don't despair though. We're going to clear it up with a little common sense.

As always, I'm only interested in your child's brilliance so that's where we're headed in this chapter.

THE FAMOUS, OR INFAMOUS, MARSHMALLOW TEST

You may have heard of the "Marshmallow Test." You can hardly walk by a discussion about children's success without tripping over it. Here's the short story: A Stanford professor and psychologist named Walter Mischel conducted a study using kids around 3 to 5 years of age (Mischel et al., "Cognitive and Attentional" 206). The kids were offered a small treat now or a larger treat later if they waited. The researchers left the room and let cameras roll to record what happened. The researchers checked up on the kids many years afterward and found that those who waited for the greater treat (delayed gratification) were doing better academically, socially, health-wise, and by several other metrics, than those who scarfed down the meager treat before more arrived (Mischel et al., "Predicting Adolescent Cognitive" 1990 982). Poof, done! If a kid has a little self-control, their future is set!

Not so fast... It's a lot more complicated than that. While seemingly everyone was focused just on the delayed gratification aspect, a few others saw it quite differently. Follow-up studies found many other very important factors that played a part in a child's ability to wait for a greater reward which they promptly used to shoot holes in the marshmallow test. Among them were how much the kids trusted the person telling them they would receive more, how much they wanted the reward, how often they had been deprived of such rewards in the past, how well they could distract themselves from thinking about the immediate treat, etc. Kind of obvious reasons, don't you think?

Socioeconomic factors have also become a concern recently when considering the marshmallow test results. In other words, if the child has been raised economically poor, the immediate reward may be taken quickly because of having lived a life of lack. Well, duh. That's a smart kid if you ask me. Of course, kids who aren't the least bit worried about where the next treat is coming from will find it easier to wait.

By the way.
The treats started as pretzels and animal crackers (Mischel and Ebbeson 332) *and then pretzels and marshmallows* (Mischel et al., "Cognitive and Attentional" 207). *Why didn't they call it the pretzel test?*

THE NEVER-ENDING DISPUTE

There's even more. First, the "Marshmallow Test" isn't a single experiment. Mischel has conducted many similar studies starting in the late 60s all the way up to 2018. There have also been countless follow-up studies by others and several studies that attempted to replicate (often with minor tweaks) Mischel's findings. Depending on who's review of those studies you read, they're either the holy grail of success or they're birdcage liner.

So, you've got multiple very viable factors being considered, you've got countless opinions and of course they all end by saying that more study is needed if we're ever to understand any of this. For crying out loud, they've had nearly 50 years. Are you getting a feeling for why I don't rely much on studies?

ARE WE WRONG ABOUT TODAY'S KIDS?

Let's confuse things a little more before we boil this down to common sense. Mischel was involved in another study that was published in 2018. This one attempted to compare kids' ability to delay gratification across multiple decades. The study found that today's kids can delay gratification longer than kids of the

60s and 80s (Carlson et al. 1395). That flies right in the face of conventional wisdom* that says living in today's instant gratification society has produced kids who can't wait a nanosecond for anything.

This study took another look at Mischel's early studies as well as a bunch of other studies, all the way up into the 2000s, including studies that attempted to replicate the marshmallow test. This study's authors (many of whom were involved in earlier studies) found that kids in the 2000s averaged delaying gratification two minutes longer than kids in the 60s and one minute longer than kids in the 80s (Carlson et al. 1395).

They theorized about what could account for this increase in ability to delay gratification saying, "Although the findings cannot be generalized to all groups of children, and the cultivation of executive function skills in the preschool period remains critically important, we speculate that increases in abstract thought and social awareness of executive function, along with rising preschool enrollment, changes in parenting, and, somewhat paradoxically, cognitive skills associated with screen technologies, may have contributed to generational improvements in the delay-of-gratification task" (Carlson et al. 1404).

Well, that makes us want to jump on the pre-school train and park our kids in front of the screens I preach against. Hang on a minute, though. Mischel has also said, when speaking of the 2018 study, "while the results indicate that the sampled children's ability to delay is not diminished on the marshmallow test, the

---

*72% of today's adults believe children cannot wait as long and 75% believe kids today have less self-control ("Can the Kids Wait" 1397).

findings do not speak to their willingness to delay gratification when faced with the proliferation of temptations now available in everyday life" ("Can the Kids Wait"). So, what the heck does that mean? Mischel is saying that the kids in the studies they analyzed can delay gratification of a particular type in a lab setting but no one knows how that translates to the real world. Of course, that can be said of almost any study.

Also, keep in mind that the kids in nearly all of the studies ranged from about three years old to six years old and they were all are believed to be middle-upper socioeconomic status (SES), although complete data is not available (Carlson et al.1401). While there appears to be improvement in the ability to delay gratification in the 80s and 2000s, we only have data up to about age six. The concern of many psychologists today is how screen use will affect children's brains in the long-term. And, by the study authors' own words, they were only speculating about the potential positive effects of screen use on the ability to delay gratification. They caution, "more research in diverse populations is needed to examine the generality of the findings and to identify causal factors" (Carlson et al. 1395).

LET'S THROW SOME COMMON SENSE ON THIS

We've had this figured out for centuries. Buyer's remorse, patience is a virtue, good things come to those who wait... Yeah, we know that being impulsive is the best path to a bad outcome. We don't need a study to tell us that. Oh, wait! I know, I know, strike while the iron's hot, the early bird gets the worm, and so on. Those can still happen without being impulsive.

We know that to do well in life, your kid needs to learn self-control and the ability to delay quick gratification in order to reap a greater reward in the long-term (think saving for retirement and not slugging someone, so you don't go to jail). And, if left on their own, most kids (and adults) will default to impulsiveness. I mean, who doesn't want what they want right now? So, it's something that is worth working on and cultivating in your child, and it definitely contributes to your pursuit of brilliance for your child.

The good news is that nearly all the researchers agree that self-control is teachable. If it weren't, how would SEC have any effect? My stance will always be to assume that it's teachable and that you should make your best effort even though there is an undeniable genetic component. The alternative is to just give up now and accept that your child's life is just one big crapshoot. I don't believe you're willing to accept that, or you wouldn't be reading this book.

The affluence quandary.
Many studies have suggested that affluent kids are better at delaying gratification and are more successful in life because they don't need to worry about where the next treat is coming from. I would charge that this is a double-edged sword. Getting everything you want instantly can, in the long term, potentially lead to that expectation and the desire for more. That's a recipe for being impulsive.

DELAYING GRATIFICATION AND BRILLIANCE

The ability to delay gratification goes hand-in-hand with brilliance. If you're smart, you will see the immediate reward, consider all your options in detail, and then make the decision that best serves your long-term goals. That's intelligent decision making in a nutshell. Even though brilliant people are fast thinkers, making a good decision often requires an investment of time and effort along with the ability to resist temptation from low hanging fruit.

The ability to delay gratification is beneficial in nearly every aspect of life. Choosing a partner, investing in education, being less susceptible to sales pitches and scams, being a better negotiator, not jumping to conclusions, being able to endure gatekeeper* classes, and making better life choices, to name a few.

*Gatekeeper class – Any dumb, useless class that is required for, but has nothing to do with, the degree you desire. Some consider the entirety of high school to be a gatekeeper class.

LET'S LOOK AT IT A DIFFERENT WAY

As with everything in this book, our goal is for this to become a natural part of your child. We want delaying gratification to be normal and just what your child does, not something that requires conscious thought and great effort to engage. Learning to delay gratification is learning to endure dissatisfaction and pain in order to have greater satisfaction and pleasure later. In other words, it's the opposite of thinking like a kid. To make that normal for your child, you're going to have to start very early, and you're going to need to be patient.

You should be realizing right now that this isn't something you should be working on with an infant. They're hungry, they cry, they want to be fed now, and they should get fed now.

HOW TO HELP YOUR CHILD IMPROVE

You and your child are going to see this process very differently. You will see yourself as being on a magnanimously self-sacrificing quest to ensure your child develops into a brilliant and successful person who will live a long life of success and happiness. Your child will see you as a sadistic dictator bent creating a world of eternal fun deprivation through your vile attempts to withhold all that is desirable in life. Even if it is for only five minutes. So, keep cool, remain the adult in the room, and don't expect instant results. Your patience is going to be vitally important as you endure copious whining, screaming, bargaining, demanding, and many other attempts by your child to circumvent your evil plan.

For most kids, this is a long-term process. Do not expect overnight results. With some kids, it can happen quickly but don't be disappointed if your child is normal and takes longer. As always, play until you win.

Let's look at what works and what doesn't:

Avoidance – This is one of the most popular ways to "teach" delayed gratification. All that's needed is to avoid temptation by hiding the goodies. Problem solved. Yay! My kid can delay gratification forever. Right, that's because there is nothing to delay. For crying out loud, this teaches your child nothing. How about we avoid this useless suggestion?

Rewarding – Another popular recommendation is to reward your child often for waiting. Maybe. That will help to build a positive association with delaying gratification which is a step in the right direction. The problem is that rewarding too often can become just another way to get a treat. Limit how often you reward to ensure that it is a teaching moment rather than just another repetition.

How often to reward is a tightrope walk. You need to reward often enough to teach that it is desirable and beneficial to wait. In the beginning, and with very small children, it's fine to create opportunities to practice. Instead of just giving the treat you already planned to give, make it a teachable moment by requiring something in return that involves a time investment, or work investment, to earn the treat. As the lesson is learned, over months and years, you need to do planned rewards less often to let delayed gratification become just another part of life.

Distraction – Some of the studies on delaying gratification found that it was more difficult for kids to resist when the adult talked up the bigger reward and the benefits of waiting. It's kind of like this: You can have this little piece of chocolate now or later you can have a huge piece of chocolate. I mean, this is going to be the most delicious, humongous piece of mouthwatering deliciousness that you've ever had in your whole life. Can you just taste that chocolate melting in your mouth...?

Of course, the kid is going to knock the researcher down getting to the piece of chocolate that's right there because the kid's mind is full of thoughts of chocolate. So, there's something to be said for keeping it real. This also tells us that getting the reward off of one's mind can increase the ability to wait. Help your child understand the benefit of waiting and then let it go as much as possible. But don't just distract your child. Explain that we're going to do something else to occupy our minds while we wait. That way your child understands the process and will have the opportunity to learn from it rather than just being distracted and unaware of the entire process.

Self-talk – Self-talk can be a distraction or an exercise in reasoning. In the original marshmallow test, it was noted that kids who engaged in self-talk were able to resist longer. Some kids sang while others made statements of affirmation along the line of, "I have to wait." We all have a dialog going in our heads. Some verbalize it, some don't. Teaching your child to talk it out can be very positive.

By the way, recent studies have indicated that people who talk to themselves tend to have higher IQs.

I prefer the reasoning aspect of self-talk. Using self-talk as a distraction is fine if the delay is going to be measured in minutes. Sometimes the delay must be much longer. Your kid can only sing for so long. Learning to reason with yourself, such as encouragement and affirmation that you're doing the right thing, is much more effective. Of course, little ones aren't going to get this right away, but this is the long-term goal.

Trust – This starts with you. You can have a huge impact on how your child views the world. Be someone your child can trust. That simply means do what you say you're going to. Of course, it's going to go wrong sometimes. When it does, own up to it boldly and do what you can to make it right. You also need to be honest. A big reason kids don't believe parents is because parents lie. "Oh, your hair is lovely with mud and grass clippings in it." When your kid asks your opinion don't give a parent answer, give an honest answer. Follow up with, "I'm not going to lie to you." Make it an event. It's not always easy. We often lie to avoid hurting our child's feelings. Do that once and you've blown it. You can be honest and gentle at the same time. Maintaining trust is tough. Getting it back is way tougher.

In the beginning, you will be doing the reasoning for your child by talking him or her through the wait. Over time hand off the reasoning to your child. Begin by asking your child questions to lead to effective self-talk. As your child gets it, sit back and let your child create the self-talk conversation.

KEEP IT REAL

We don't always get what we want. That can cause even us adults to abandon what otherwise was a good plan. Delaying gratification can sometimes lead to a "when you snooze, you lose" situation. Yup, that's life, and it's important that your child learns that. It's up to you to explain it. However, never let this happen when you are the one promising the loot! Maintaining your child's trust is way too important to let that happen. Sure, you're going to fail to deliver sometimes, but that's for big things that will happen later in life when your child is more emotionally equipped to understand. There's no excuse for not delivering on the bigger piece of cake you promised when your kid is just a tot.

YOU'RE TEACHING TWO TYPES

Delayed gratification can be divided into two types, short-term and long-term. Short term events are of the "be good, and you'll get to play longer" variety. Long-term events can include things like "skip spending your money on junk and you can buy a new bike." You need to teach both.

Short-term - Start small and keep it brief. Also, keep it relevant. I like silliness for teaching but, in this case, it's important to keep it realistic. Making up superfluous reasons to wait detracts from the reasons for delaying. Sure, create reasons but just keep them relevant to your child's life. You can make the waits longer as your child progresses.

Long-term – This is difficult to teach a small child because their world is wrapped up in now. Very young children are not designed to be long-term thinkers. Still, there are going to be events in your child's life that involve long-term thinking so use them to your advantage. Saving up for a big vacation, not seeing the grandparents for just a weekend when you can make the trip later for a whole week, planning for that first pet, are good examples. Keep it age-appropriate and explain and encourage along the way.

ORDER THINGS THE OLD-FASHIONED WAY

When I was a kid, every cereal box prize took six to eight weeks just to ship. The wait was tough, but it was also expected. Looking back, though, it was the anticipation that was often greater than the prize. There's just something really great about anticipating the arrival of something that you've earned (by saving box tops) and that you've made happen yourself (by filling out the order form and mailing it).

Find a way to make this happen for your child. Of course, this is for an older child who can understand the process. There are still plenty of things you can order that take time. It's very important that your child is involved in the order process. Make sure it's going to take a minimum of two to three weeks to arrive. Books are great because you can select media mail as the shipping method. That always takes more time. Order something from around the globe and select the cheapest shipping method. And no tracking! Keep its arrival time a mystery.

Another great way to do this is to find an old-fashioned pen pal from across one of the big ponds. If you have friends or family a long way away who have children let them in on the plan. This is an easy way to set up a safe pen pal relationship. If it seems the letters are arriving too quickly just hold them a little while before mailing. You know, just be a devious parent.

A HUGE LESSON FOR THE FUTURE

This is loosely related to delayed gratification but very worth the time. This doesn't apply to very young children so, if you need to, keep it in reserve for later years.

My brother is five years older than I am. When he was 14, he decided to give up sodas for a year. I'm not sure why he did it, but it became a serious challenge he set for himself. Over that year, he bitterly refused anything that even resembled a soda. Keep in mind that he liked sodas just as much as any other kid and he met tons of temptation along the way. He persevered, though, and made it through the year without even a sip of soda.

Accomplishing something like this is huge for a kid. The benefits are enumerable. Setting a seemingly insurmountable challenge for one's self and meeting the challenge is a massive self-confidence boost. Seeing the look of disbelief on the faces of those you have to explain it too along the way bolsters that sense of accomplishment all the more. More importantly, the entire process is a continual lesson in self-control.

I followed my brother's lead a few years later and also gave up sodas for a year. I've even done this as an adult too having given up sodas for many years and various other things for a year or so at a time. I've actually given up coffee for a year more than once. I believe that alone confirms my superhuman credentials.

This has paid off for me many times in real terms too. In October 1996, I learned that the consumption of beef and pork was contributing to health problems I was experiencing. Now keep in mind that I was very much a steak and potatoes guy. The short story is that I haven't had a bite of beef or pork since, and that was over 23 years ago. This has been extremely difficult, but I've never given in for even a single bite. That would have been impossible without the self-control lessons that started with just giving up a treat for a while.

So, help your older child select something to give up. This is definitely a brilliance builder. It doesn't have to be for an entire year, although that would be great. Maybe for a month, even just a week. It must be something that will be missed. Giving up liver and onions is not going to cut it. Make it hurt a little.

If your kid fails, don't make a big deal of it. Just encourage trying again and be supportive. Never, show disappointment or ridicule your child for failing. This isn't easy after all. Tell your kid to always play until you win. You've never truly failed until you quit trying.

THE BOTTOM LINE

Brilliance requires self-control, the ability to delay gratification, and the fortitude to deal with discomfort and disappointment. Don't let anyone tell you that your child is incapable of learning this difficult skill. Start early, keep it age and maturity-level-appropriate, and be patient. Even small gains are worth the effort.

10

THE SIMPLE STUFF

Sometimes it's the little things that make you brilliant.

PERCEPTION IS REALITY FOR MOST FOLKS. And, it's a two-sided coin. On one side, if you're the only one with the answer, no matter how simple the question, you're the smart one in the room. On the other side, if you're the only one who can't answer the simple question, you're the dumb one. Yeah, that's not a dignified way to say it, and it may not be fair, but it's often true. If you are unaware of basic information, which it seems today most people are, you can't possibly appear intelligent much less brilliant.

I was in the hallway of our local community college waiting for my then 15-year-old daughter. She was taking the college's entrance exam, which she blasted right to the top of the charts, by the way. I was approached by three young ladies who appeared to be in their early twenties. One spoke up loudly and urgently saying, "I need you to settle an argument!" She pointed to the other two and went on to say, "Tell them that a quarter after means twenty-five minutes after!" Now, most people would immediately label her as dumb. That's not possible because she has the same brain capacity as anyone else. But she sure sounded dumb. I broke the news to her as respectfully and gently as I could, but her two friends were laughing their heads off.

Do you really want your child to be the one who can't make change for a dollar, doesn't know how many ounces are in a pound, can't mentally add two two-digit numbers, and who doesn't know 1/8" from 1/16"? If you're the only person in the room who can add two three-digit numbers in your head or who knows the difference between antiperspirant and deodorant, you're the brilliant person in the room. Really, it doesn't take much to be considered brilliant. Unfortunately, it takes much less to be considered dumb.

WHAT'S GOING ON...

Fundamental abilities are extremely important. Equally important is knowing what's going on in the world and how the world works. If you're the only one at the water cooler who has no idea who the sitting president is, that we live in a republic rather than a democracy, and that the boss retired two months ago, you're not going to be thought of as intelligent and definitely not brilliant.

The habit of being aware starts now. And the knowledge base that will be necessary to understand and relate to more and more complex situations begins now. Keep it age-appropriate but keep your kid informed and find every way possible to keep your child engaged. Even the very little ones can know why there's a mayor, why we pay taxes, the basics of what's in the news, etc. They don't need to see the terrible and ugly side of society just yet, but they can begin to understand the players and how society works.

If you don't think this is important, just find an average twenty-something and start asking some very basic history questions. You just can't appear brilliant without a rudimentary understanding of the world in which you live.

ONCE AGAIN, SCHOOL IS NOT THE ANSWER

School is not going to fix this for you. Sure, in kindergarten kids are taught some of the basics like measuring and such. School will also tell kids a little about government and history and the like, but it's all done in lesson form. That rarely penetrates to the level of subconscious proficiency. These basic skills must become natural to your child. More importantly, the desire and expectancy to know them must become a natural part of your child. That's what develops awareness. School and disjointed, impractical, study-for-the-test lessons will never do that. Just living it day to day will.

WHY GRANDPA CAN'T USE THE TV REMOTE

This is a little off the subject of the simple stuff, but it's still a very important concept to understand when it comes to being able to do the simple stuff in adulthood.

Using a TV remote is easy. Even one of those multi-unit jobs that can control the TV, the DVD player, the cable box, and a couple of other gizmos. You simply select the device and then logically work through the menu system on that device to navigate to what you need. Piece of cake. It's easy for you because the remote, and all of the devices it controls, employ control setups that are generally similar and are just a progression from simpler devices you've used your whole life.

Easy for you to say. Grandpa didn't even have a TV as a kid, and the console unit he cherished through early adulthood required a ten-foot hike across the living room just to spin the dial to one of the other three channels available. Not to mention the required adjustment to the rabbit ears.

The point is that Grandpa has no base knowledge of the thinking processes involved in using technology. We learn the basics in childhood and then work our way up progressively. We develop thought processes and understanding that spans across similar intellectual demands.

The problem for Grandpa is that he let his knowledge base stay right where it has always been. He never bothered with learning that new-fangled junk, and now he stares at the remote like it's an alien device while chanting his mantra of, "I don't know, I don't know..."

This doesn't go for just tech. Everything to do with functioning in our society requires base knowledge acquired at a young age that sets the stage for lifetime skill acquisition.

THIS IS EASY

There's nothing to it. Just teach your children the simple, everyday, commonsense knowledge and skills that everyone needs to get by. Relearn them yourself if necessary. No one will ever know. Just carry your laptop into the closet in the middle of the night and study up.

Now don't start planning a class on this. Do you hear me, homeschoolers? And don't make a big deal of it either. Just make it a natural part of your day every time you have the opportunity.

Whatever you're doing, have your child help. Explain to them the details as they're helping. If it's measuring that you're doing, explain as you're using the ruler, measuring tape, or measuring cup. Ask your child to complete the task for you as much as possible on their own and encourage your child to ask questions. Make it fun and light. Most importantly, make it obvious to your child that they're doing something important. Kids love that feeling.

THIS IS NOT A ONCE AND DONE DEAL

You've got to make this a habit. That means start now and never quit. We're all rushed and often don't have time to have our children involved because we just need to get things done. Believe me, I know because I'm guilty of this one. So, it's been that way in the past. Big deal. You can't start any earlier than now. Get on with it. Oh yeah, and be very, very patient. Your child will pick up on tension like a gnat smelling potato salad. If you're lucky, that will send your child packing for just the moment. More likely it's going to sink right down into the subconscious and begin to create a negative association with the subject, the process, and you. We don't want that, right? If things get frustrating just bail out for a while and start again later.

THE PROBLEM WITH LESSONS

Lessons are an interruption for a kid. They're something that kids just force themselves through while thinking about what they would rather be doing so they can actually go do what they would rather be doing. No real learning happens for a kid during a lesson. Why do you think those lessons are filled with so much repetition? If the method was effective, kids would learn in half the time. Just notice how many times they have to be shown how to use a complicated video game. And, while we're on the subject, why do you think it takes fourteen years (K4 – 12) to graduate a kid who can't read or make change for a buck? Again, it could easily be done in less than half the time (complete with reading ability) but then what would we do with a bunch of eight and nine-year-old high school graduates?

WHEN TO START

That crib isn't going to assemble itself; you know. Okay, that's a little young, but start as young as possible. Begin by giving your child toy versions of tools, utensils, money, devices, etc. Anything that fits into everyday life. Later, under your supervision, introduce your kid to the real thing. Again, as early as possible (no choking hazards for the little ones!).

This early thing isn't limited to jobs and the like. Include your child in discussions about life and the world too. Meter it out in kid-appropriate terms but get them involved early. Let them in on discussions between you and others as well. With a nod and a wink, ensure that other adults know to keep it in kid terms. My brother and I preferred the company of adults from the time we were six or seven years old. I know you're not going to be bothered by having your child involved, or you wouldn't be reading this book in the first place, right?

WHAT TO TEACH

Here are just a few ideas to get you started. The possibilities are limitless. Be sure to include things that you foresee being improved upon in the future, so you begin to build relevant base knowledge now.

The World - Tell your kid about world events, in kid terms, of course.

Measuring - Teach your kid to measure everything from distance to volume and in multiple standards.

Money - Teach money basics (you know, how to count change) including finance, mortgages, and taxes.

Simple Math - Encourage your child to do mental math. Calculators are for the difficult stuff only. Estimation skills are extremely important too.

For mental math, add differently.

Teach your child to add from left to right. Think about how you count money. We always count the large bills first and work our way down to the 1s. Counting the 1s first would require much more mental effort as you carry from the 1s to the 10s to the 100s. Give it a try. 452 + 674. Mentally follow along. 400 + 600 is 1000. Looking at the next column add 50 to equal 1050 add 70 is 1120 then as you see the 1s 1122, 1126. Of course, school is going to require your child to know the slow difficult way too. You know, ***"SHOW YOUR WORK!"***

Grammar - Use and require something close to proper grammar (it doesn't have to be perfect). Want to sound dumb quick? Just blurt out a double negative or two, put "then" where "than" belongs, write "should of" instead of "should've" and say "orientated" instead of "oriented."

How To Fix Stuff - Teach your kid general home and automobile maintenance. This can be fun, and it will serve your kid well.

Medicine – Teach things like why you don't take OTC (over the counter) sleeping pills and antihistamines together. Hint, they're often the same thing. Double dosing is a bad thing. Think about how different things would be if the general public had understood antibiotics many years ago. Teach why we must understand what we put into our bodies.

Reading - Ensure that your child is a fluent reader. Learning is incredibly easier when one can read effortlessly. That greases the skids for brilliance. Don't wait for school. Find a good phonics-based system and get on with it.

Vocabulary - A powerful vocabulary screams brilliance. Start very early. No lessons. Just use the words and wait for questions.

Manners - The all-powerful manners. After proper grammar, having good manners is the easiest way to appear brilliant.

Self-control - Calm under pressure. Ever watch a movie where everyone's panicking? Who's the leader? The in-control smart person, of course.

Cooking – Cooking includes measuring, math, time management, very basic chemistry, and much more. It's a basic stuff mecca.

THE BOTTOM LINE

Include your kid in your life and what you do. Be patient and welcome questions and participation. Even if it makes the job take much longer. And no lessons!

11

THE HIGH-LEVEL STUFF

Your child is capable of much more than you think.

EVEN IF YOU BELIEVE YOUR KID IS A GENIUS, you're probably still underestimating your child's mental abilities. Don't get me wrong here. I believe it is a huge mistake to expect children to live with their noses stuck in books 24/7 with the goal of entering Harvard at age 12. Kids need to have a childhood. On the other hand, there is no need to constantly dumb everything down either. We dumb things down way too far for kids.

Let's take dinosaurs as an example. What kid doesn't love dinosaurs? My son and daughter were nearly obsessed with dinosaurs in their toddler years. I remember a relative visiting during that time. We'll call her Jane. My then three-year-old daughter (she may have actually been younger) broke out her collection of dinos to proudly show Jane. Jane was delighted to join in. Jane picked one up and said, "I like this green one." To which my daughter replied, "That's a pachycephalosaurs." She continued on to properly name each of the dinos in her rather large collection and provided in-depth details about each as well. My kids knew the proper names of dozens of dinosaurs when they were two years old. It was extremely easy for them. They would also be quick to correct you if you mentioned a brontosaurus that never actually existed. Look it up. They could also go into great detail about each dino in scientific terms. My kids are not special. Any kid can do this. Just give it a try, be patient, and make it fun. Interestingly, they will pick up quickly on the fact that this is not typical kid knowledge which will make it all the more fun for them. Fun always gets you in through the VIP entrance.

NEVER OVERDO IT

You should never demand that your child absorb advanced information. Just provide them the information as long as they will take the bait. A little encouragement is fine as long as there are no demands or pressure. Keep it fun, give them a pat on the back, and see how far it goes. If they lose interest, drop it for a while. If they engage in conversation or debate, keep it going. The more interactive the conversation, the more your child will absorb. You will also be displaying confidence in your child, and that is gold for future learning and your relationship.

You're never going to make this happen if your child is living on a steady diet of screen time and mindless video games. Really, ditch that junk right now. It's conditioning your child to live for entertainment, and it's stiff competition for the things of value that you're trying to impart to your child. And that competition is why you must keep this light and fun. Your ace in the hole is that, as I said earlier, your child will quickly pick up on the fact that this is "privileged" information for a kid. Use that to your advantage to keep your kid motivated. Keep it all very positive and even invite your kid to show off a little. Show me a kid that doesn't like being the center of attention every now and then. Remember, keep it fun, very fun.

Okay, I know, some kids are uncomfortable with that kind of attention (that describes both of mine). But they still like it when you express confidence in them. You know your kid. Do it on your child's terms. Email, a social media post, whatever works. The last thing you want to do is alienate your child.

WHY BOTHER?

Let's talk a little more about my kids and dinos. First, dino names are a great way to work on your child's speech. The names can be very challenging to pronounce. Your child will voluntarily work very hard to learn them. If you can't pronounce them yourself, watch a couple of documentaries. You'll get it. It's also a great memory exercise, and it's fun (remember the privileged info thing). And it doesn't have to be dinos. If your kid likes something different, by all means, use that. This is about expanding your child's mind, knowledge, and abilities, not dinos.

There are other reasons that are much more important. As I said earlier, you're expressing great confidence in your child when you teach them higher-level information. They pick up on that very quickly. It gives them a great sense of accomplishment and it creates very powerful positive subjective memories. It also increases their base knowledge level upon which everything else is built. The greater one's base knowledge, the easier it is to retain and understand future knowledge due to the ability to relate the two. All memory is relative. It also makes your kid feel outstanding. Kids love the reaction they get from adults who can't keep up. I mean, how cool is that?

A LITTLE DETAIL, PLEASE

Let's understand better what we're doing here. You simply don't need to always dumb it down for your child. Tell your child how things work. Let them ask questions. Give them simplified and detailed explanations slowly and incrementally. As long as they keep taking the bait, why withhold information from them? Of course, you must keep it appropriate, and you can't tell them something that may lead to an unsafe situation.

A WORD OF CAUTION

Never teach a young child how to do something dangerous. The little buggers like to try everything and usually in the worst place at the worst time. Keep everyone safe.

TEACH THEM WHAT YOU KNOW AND DO

That's a great place to start. It tells your child more about you, and they get to learn. You'll be amazed at how quickly they catch on. If this is new, it may be a little rocky at first. Give it time and persist. Always play until you win. But never keep playing if your child is frustrated. And don't take it personally if your child gets bored. After all, boredom is your child's stock-in-trade.

DON'T WAIT FOR SCHOOL TO DO IT

Waiting for school misses on two fronts. First, you miss out on that unbelievably valuable time you have with your child before losing them, for hours a day, to school. And, second, school isn't going to do it.

Don't let them stop you either. Some teachers can't stand it when a kid is ahead of the class. Too bad. Tell the teacher to deal with it. Period.

AT WHAT AGE?

I can't tell you to make what you teach your child age-appropriate. That would be counter to the entire premise of this chapter. Your child does need to be somewhat ready, though. That means that your child needs to have base knowledge upon which to build this new structure of knowledge. Explaining organic chemistry to a one-year-old is probably not going to be very successful.

You know your child better than anyone. If you don't know, you're quickly going to find out once you begin. Just pay attention to how well your child understands and adjust when necessary.

12

QUIET TIME

Being bored is a good thing.

HALLELUJAH! THIS GUY IS FINALLY SINGING my song. Heck yeah, I need some quiet time. Just tell me how long I can lock the kid in the basement so I can break out the wine! Well... it isn't quite like that. But it seems that almost everyone who writes about quiet time for children is saying just that, albeit a little more gently.

You are important, and of course, you need a break from time to time. Kids can be a little demanding. Maybe the word I'm looking for is "unrelenting." Regardless, you're the adult in the room, and I'm only interested in your child's brain. Sorry.

In addition to giving mommy (they never mention dad) time for a break, most of what has been written about quiet time is about how it gives your little one time to recharge and how it encourages autonomy and the like. They often suggest creating a space in your home where you can plunk your kid down with a box of toys so you can get out of dodge to let your little one explore the independent life. Yeah, kids need to learn to be independent and such, but I'm not the one who's going to encourage you to plot ways to be away from your child. If anything, I want you involved with your child more than you are now. And, as I said above, I'm only interested in your child's intelligence.

So, I'm not interested in planned quiet sessions or forced isolation (yup, no basement lockups). Kids are more likely to interpret a planned quiet session as an interruption to their day at the least and more likely as punishment. Resistance isn't going to make for very quiet quiet time.

As for the box of toys suggestion. Absolutely. I'm all for giving your child toys during quiet time. That is if they're the right kind. More on that below.

WHAT'S SO GREAT ABOUT QUIET TIME?

Quiet time is absolutely essential to your child's mind, brain, and brilliance. We live in a very noisy, busy world. And we want our children to learn and to be successful so we fill every spare minute with educational toys, activities, alphabet practice time, and anything else we can teach them. That's on top of all of the other noise of the day. Bravo for your enthusiasm and interest, but for your child to learn more, you need to do a little less.

Your child is a little learning machine that is hungry for data and experiences. It's all being absorbed at breakneck speed, and your kid will go until face-planting on the carpet. Kids' brains begin to misfire from fatigue and overload long before they realize it. Quiet time is essential for combating the negative effects of our busy world as well as for basic elements of brilliance.

JUST A FEW OF THE BENEFITS OF QUIET TIME:

Some of these will benefit your child now, some of them will benefit your child later in life.

Epiphanies - Quiet time is when epiphanies occur. Epiphanies can take many forms, but they are typically flashes of valuable insight for problem-solving or sudden answers to failed attempts at recall. Epiphanies are the result of your subconscious mind getting the job done in the background and then sending a flare up to alert your conscious mind. When your conscious mind is churning away, it tends to take over and never gives your subconscious mind a chance to get a thought in edgewise.

Quiet time lets you hear from your subconscious mind. Think about it. How many times have you been quietly doing something when you have a sudden long-sought-after answer pop into your mind? Let your conscious mind keep screaming away, and those epiphanies will go unheard. Your child's brilliance depends heavily on these epiphanies. Now, while your child is very young, is the time to develop comfort and appreciation for quiet time that will yield those epiphanies later in life.

Imagination – Quiet time is when your child's mind can wander, play, and experiment. Brilliant creations of the mind happen when the mind is free. Of course, a bunch of dumb useless stuff happens too. You have to take the bad with the good. The point is that the good isn't going to happen at all if the imagination is left to wither in the shadow of a constantly churning conscious mind. During quiet time, other people and devices are not doing the creating and thinking for your child. Your child is doing it. That has a massive positive impact on brilliance.

Memory – You just can't remember as well if you are constantly receiving input. Your child's brain needs downtime for processing. Most memory processing happens during sleep, but wakeful time is powerful as well. Us adults can use quiet time to ponder and enhance our awareness of newly encountered information. Kids don't consciously work to understand and build memory associations. Quiet time handles it for them. Developing comfort with quiet time now can make it more comfortable and desirable later in life. Developing the habit of quiet time now will enhance memory now and for a lifetime.

Being calm – The world is full of stress, and stress can put brilliance in a chokehold. Learning to calm one's self during quiet time can be extraordinarily helpful when coping with a demanding world.

Mental fatigue – Your kid's brain needs a break. Nuff said.

Ability to shut down – Sometimes, it's necessary to shut down completely. Anyone who can't sleep for thinking about their to-do list gets this. Quiet time is a great step toward learning to control one's self. That self-control will come in handy as an adult, and even in the school years when the ability to shut down is a necessity.

QUIET TIME DEFINED

The quiet time I'm concerned with is time away from stimulus and anything that does the thinking and creating for your child. That does not mean sitting motionless or being isolated, although that's okay if your kid is good with it. Quietly playing with simple toys fits the bill perfectly. I do prefer silence though. That means a silent room, not a silent child. I often kept classical music playing when my kids were little, but quiet time needs to be as void of outer stimulus as possible. So, tell Mozart to take five.

By the way.
I didn't play Mozart due to the much-ballyhooed IQ boosting benefits that were all the rage a few years ago. That theory is heavily disputed and most likely bunk. I played Mozart because I like it, and I hoped to develop in my kids an appreciation for dignified and intricate music.

WHAT QUIET TIME IS NOT

Quiet time does not mean *forcing* your child to sit still quietly. To be effective, quiet time must be free of threats, force, and punishment. Bribery, in the form of snacks or an interesting new (simple) toy, on the other hand, while not optimal, is acceptable. At least in the beginning.

WHAT HAPPENS DURING QUIET TIME?

Lots of things. Your child may sit quietly. Great. More likely there's going to be lots of imaginative play. That's great too. If your child falls asleep, so be it. We'll try again next time.

Here's how it works. Ahead of time, you've amassed a collection of appropriate toys. Things like, blocks, stuffed animals, toy furniture, toy farms, toy animals, toy people, cars and trucks, washable markers, paints (if you're ready for the cleanup), crayons, lots of paper, things that can be taken apart and put back together, boxes of various sizes, paper towel tubes, and anything else that requires imagination to use. These may be kept in a specific area or they can be deployed wherever you happen to be.

Ensure that all the toys are safe. No choke hazards!

Sit your kid down and let play happen. Pretend play, making the animals talk, breaking things, mixing up the parts, and anything else that requires imagination and hands-on experience is perfect. Again, your child does not need to be isolated. Sit right there with your kid and enjoy. You may even need to give a suggestion or two to get things rolling. Offer up a scenario for the toy people or suggest building something with a few select items. Then, as much as possible, sit back and let it happen. Having another kid involved occasionally is good too. Imagination unfolds exponentially when two kids are working together. Alone or with another kid, it may get loud, but it still qualifies as quiet time if the noise is coming from within your child.

Tip

Take advantage of times like hours in a waiting room, when you're talking to a friend, or when you've had it up to here with your overly energetic bundle of joy, to give your child a powerful brilliance building experience. Sit your child down beside you. Then break out your smartphone, tablet, or laptop. Then let your kiddo watch you power the thing down and put it away. I mean out of sight away. Flush it down a toilet if that's what's necessary to prevent you from pulling it out again. Now, tell your child to play. Better yet, you play along too.

THOSE "EDUCATIONAL" TOYS

Get rid of those "educational" toys. All of them (almost). Most of them are not educational anyway. They're just beeping, musical pieces of junk that try to fool you into thinking they're educational. There are some exceptions that we will get to below. For the most part, though, kids are like cats. The box is usually way more interesting than the piece of junk that came in it. For kids, the box is way better for them as well.

Experiences that involve touching, smelling, tasting, and hearing are what will help your child develop brilliance. Your child needs to do things. Simple as that. Your child needs to create, experiment, experience, succeed, and fail. So-called educational shows, videos, apps, and toys that do the thinking and creating for your child are worthless. Your child is just living someone else's imagination. That's nearly useless to your child's brain and intelligence development. Also, we're trying to avoid external stimulus and informational input.

This is why most so-called educational toys are off-limits for quiet time. It would be better if they were off-limits permanently. However, there is a grey area in the educational toy sector. Most of these are for toddlers or older kids. They include interconnecting blocks, kits to build specific things such as cars, and skill-building toys (think crochet and musical instruments). These toys are usually very narrow in scope. Save them for later when your child is developing specific interests such as science or a specific artistic modality. Right now, we need wide open imagination at the wheel. Your very young child is getting plenty of data to work with from the immediately surrounding world that is plenty new. Those narrow scope science and construction kits are fine for non-quiet time activities, though.

SCREENS

I said a lot about screens back in chapter 3. If you need a refresher, head back there now for the details. Right now, I need you to understand that screens are the mortal enemy of quiet time.

Get rid of the screens during quiet time. All of them. TV, phones, pads, tablets, all of them. Heck, even cover the one on the fridge (on the fridge, really?). You don't have to get rid of them permanently. Just every moment that you're with your little child. That includes your phone. Okay, the occasional business call might be okay, but keep it short and then get back to your kid.

SPEND LESS TIME BEING ENTERTAINED

This subject only loosely fits in the quiet time discussion, but it's important none the less. Want to lose your imaginative and thinking skills? Just let someone, or some piece of technology, do your thinking for you. Yup, that goes for creative skills as well as logic and deductive abilities.

Creative abilities take the biggest hit from constantly being entertained because your child is passively living someone else's imagination and letting their own sit on the sidelines. Cognitive abilities suffer because of the massive time dedicated to vegging in front of mindless content. Then there's all the tech that handles simple math and the like. Intellectual apathy and atrophy are the results. As I keep saying, your child needs to accomplish and create rather than always experiencing someone else's accomplishments.

HOW TO MAKE IT HAPPEN

At the beginning of this chapter, I said I'm not interested in planned quiet sessions. Well, yeah, you do actually need to plan. You just don't want your kid to know it's planned. Just don't plan to jerk your kid out of what they're doing and switch the kid to quiet time like turning out a light. That's a recipe for rebellion. Lead or even trick your child into it. Better yet, take advantage of any opening your kids gives you in the form of slowing down a bit. Seize the moment and gently transition your little one into quiet time.

Turn off the input and the stimulus. If you've already let your kid get hooked on a digital pacifier, that's going to be tough, but it has to happen. The earlier the better. If your child is already addicted, which can be truly determined only by a professional trained in that area, you're going to need professional help breaking that addiction. Find that help and take advantage of it now.

If your child is very young, you can just hold your child in a silent room. Speak softly. Play with your child gently and just leave the surrounding world out for a while.

MY CHILD QUIET? YOU'RE OUT OF YOUR MIND.

You're probably thinking I'm crazy for believing that your little tricycle motor is ever going to be quiet and awake at the same time. The good news is that it doesn't take a lot of quiet time to be beneficial. There are no hard and fast standards or numbers to go by. Every kid is different. Start where you are, try to build to more and more time, and be patient if it doesn't go well. Really, a full minute might be the max for some kids when starting. Five minutes is really great and is a good sign that things are working. Five minutes three times during the day is wonderful. Fifteen minutes in a session is spectacular. You're the expert on your child. Just watch, listen, and constantly work to improve.

AT THE RISK OF SOUNDING LIKE A PARENTING LECTURE...

I talked earlier about the need for you to have a break. Absolutely, you need a break from time to time and sleep and help. Just never, ever let your child know that he or she is the source of your need for that break. Your child isn't a little adult and will not process the news logically. Your child can very easily interpret your need for a break as rejection or as a statement about their worth, etc.

It's a sure bet your child will take it personally, if only at a subjective level. Pitch the break as a positive for your child. "Mommy (or Daddy) is going to give you some time to make something wonderful out of these blocks," or "I want you to draw me a picture of our cat," or "We want you to paint the garage," whatever. I'm not saying you need to sugarcoat everything you say to your child. Just choose your words with your child's perception in mind. And if you've reached that point that we all reach from time to time, have someone else do it, or wait until you've regained your composure.

THE BOTTOM LINE

Your kid's brain needs quiet time. That goes for all ages and stages. Memory, problem-solving, and nearly every aspect of your child's brilliance depends on it. Heck, your brain needs quiet time too.

Make quiet time happen and make it as palatable and attractive to your child as possible. Make it a normal part of your and your child's day every day. No fanfare, no demands, and no this-is-a-lesson attitude. It's just what you do.

Understand that quiet time doesn't necessarily need to be quiet, and it certainly doesn't require isolation. Quiet time just means that your child's brain gets a break from the mental demands of new information and stimulation. You can never go wrong with old-school, very basic toys.

Your constant goal is for your child to welcome quiet time throughout school and into adulthood where the demands are greater, the input is more voluminous, and epiphanies have greater value.

MOVING ON FROM HERE

This is all useless unless you can put it to work.

DON'T GET CAUGHT UP IN THE INTRICACIES

The priority is to enjoy life with your little one. Everyone's probably warning you about how quickly this time passes. Listen to them. They're right.

You might be overwhelmed raising a little one or two or three. Now, you're even more overwhelmed because of all this stuff you've learned that you need to do to help your child become brilliant.

Take a breath. Let it happen. Pick something to work on and find a way to fit it into the day in a relaxed and fun way. Later, add something else. Before you know it, you'll be living life the brilliant way.

I will leave you with these bits of advice:
>Slow down and enjoy time with your child.
>Get down on the floor with your kid and be a kid.
>Ditch screens whenever and wherever possible.
>Look your kid in the eye with your full attention.
>Play, play, play, and play with purpose.
>Expect difficulties, deal with them, then move on.
>Take school seriously but take education more seriously.
>Let your kid help no matter how inconvenient.
>Let your kid be a kid.
>Always remember that your kid is not a little adult.
>Expect a lot but be happy with what you get.

Always remember that your very young child has no concept of the value of your things, how bad your day was, or why we can't have ice cream for dinner. Or can we...?

BIBLIOGRAPHY

Bilton N. "Steve Jobs Was a Low-Tech Parent." *The New York Times*, 10 Sept. 2014, https://www.nytimes.com/2014/09/11/fashion/steve-jobs-apple-was-a-low-tech-parent.html.

"Can the Kids Wait? Today's Youngsters May Be Able to Delay Gratification Longer Than Those of the 1960's." *American Psychological Association*, 25 June 2018, https://www.apa.org/news/press/releases/2018/06/delay-gratification.

Carlson S. M., et al. "Cohort Effects in Children's Delay of Gratification." *American Psychological Association*, vol. 54, no. 8, 2018, pp. 1395-1407, http://dx.doi.org/10.1037/dev0000533.

Glass, David C., et al. "Behavioral Consequences of Adaptation to Controllable and Uncontrollable Noise." *Journal of Experimental Social Psychology*, 7, 1971, pp. 244-257.

Glass, David C., et al. "Psychic Cost of Adaptation to an Environmental Stressor." *Journal of Personality and Social Psychology*, vol. 12, no. 3, 1969, pp. 200-210.

Klein, Richard A., et al. "Many Labs 2: Investigating Variation in Replicability Across Samples and Settings." *Advances in Methods and Practices in Psychological Science*, vol. 1, no. 4, Dec. 2018, pp. 443–490, doi:10.1177/2515245918810225.

Mischel, Walter, et al. "Cognitive and Attentional Mechanisms in Delay of Gratification." *Journal of Personality and Social Psychology*, vol. 21, no. 2, 1972, pp. 204-218.

Mischel. Walter, et al. "Predicting Adolescent Cognitive and Self-Regulatory Competencies From Preschool Delay of Gratification: Identifying Diagnostic Conditions." *Developmental Psychology*, vol. 26, no. 6, 1990, pp. 978-986.

Mischel, Walter and Ebbe B. Ebbesen. "Attention in Delay of Gratification." *Journal of Personality and Social Psychology*, vol. 16, no. 2, 1970, pp. 329-337.

Made in the USA
Columbia, SC
03 August 2020

14324982R00093